THE
ETHIOPIAN
CAMPAIGN
AND
FRENCH
POLITICAL
THOUGHT

THE ETHIOPIAN CAMPAIGN AND FRENCH POLITICAL THOUGHT

YVES R. SIMON

Translated by

ROBERT ROYAL

Edited by

ANTHONY O. SIMON

Foreword by

A. JAMES MCADAMS

University of Notre Dame Press
Notre Dame, Indiana

Manufactured in the United States of America

Library of Congress Cataloging-in-Publication Data

Simon, Yves René Marie, 1903–1961.
    [Campagne d'Éthiopie et la pensée politique française. English]
  The Ethiopian campaign and French political thought /
Yves R. Simon ; translated by Robert Royal ;
edited by Anthony O. Simon ; foreword by A. James McAdams.
      p. cm.
    Includes bibliographical references and index.
    ISBN-13: 978-0-268-04130-4 (paper : alk. paper)
    ISBN-10: 0-268-04130-X (paper : alk. paper)
  1. Italo-Ethiopian War, 1935–1936—Foreign public opinion, French.
2. Italo-Ethiopian War, 1935–1936—Moral and ethical aspects.
3. France—Relations—Italy. 4. Italy—Relations—France.
5. Intellectuals—France—Political activity—History—20th century.
6. Public opinion—France—History—20th century. 7. Italo-Ethiopian
War, 1935–1936—Diplomatic history. 8. League of Nations—History.
9. Just war doctrine—Case studies. 10. Preemptive attack (Military
science)—Case studies. I. Royal, Robert, 1949– II. Simon, Anthony O.
III. Title.
    DT387.8.s513   2009
    963'.056—dc22

                    2009021902

CONTENTS

FOREWORD

There are at least two features of Yves Simon's *The Ethiopian Campaign and French Political Thought* that may initially strike the reader as curious. The first is that Simon does not begin this short but trenchant and thought-provoking study with an examination of Benito Mussolini's attempt in October 1935 to restore Italy's national pride by declaring war on Ethiopia. Instead, he starts with the incendiary cause célèbre of late-nineteenth-century French politics, the so-called Dreyfus Affair. What does an innocent French army captain's conviction for treason in 1894 have to do with a military campaign that took place in 1935? The second mystery has to do with Simon himself. Why should a thinker who is now regarded as among the preeminent Thomistic philosophers and political theorists of the twentieth century have devoted one of his earliest books, following two philosophical treatises on metaphysics and moral knowledge, to a specific event in international politics?

The answer to both questions can be found in Simon's upbringing and intellectual milieu. Simon was born into a wealthy industrial family that combined a deep Catholic faith with strong republican convictions. As a youth, Simon was also influenced by the horror of war. One of his brothers was killed when his plane was shot down over Germany in 1917. Yet it was not this loss in itself that shaped his thinking about later events, including Mussolini's Ethiopian adventure. Like other members of his family, Simon was a patriot and considered it an honor to fight and die for France. Indeed, the only thing that kept him from enlisting was the fact that he had been severely handicapped by tuberculosis as a youth. Rather, his family's political and religious sentiments and an early fascination with the anarchistic populism of Pierre-Joseph Proudhon led him to distrust the intentions of all politicians and their allies. In Simon's eyes, the unfounded accusations against a Jewish military officer, Alfred Dreyfus, proved that these suspicions were warranted. Furthermore, the French government's subsequent efforts to cover up the scandal and downplay its anti-Semitic and hypernationalistic roots demonstrated that France's commitment to republican values was tenuous at best. Under these circumstances, one could never take the protection of personal liberties and human dignity for granted.

Simon's engagement in these issues was by no means atypical. In the aftermath of World War I, an entire generation of French intellectuals had arisen that was characterized by the desire to combine the hard facts of politics with the pursuit of the highest human ideals. Today, this disposition might be attributed to the so-called "public intellectual," but Simon's generation was much more than that. For the sophisticated man or woman of ideas in the 1920s and 1930s, a thorough immersion in the political and social questions of the day was a way of life. Educated Parisians read five or six newspapers a day—*Le Figaro*, the ultranationalist *Action française*, the liberal Catholic 7 *"Sept"*, and many others. Parisians could be counted upon to comment authoritatively on an array of opinions surrounding pressing domestic and international issues. And they did so with gusto.

The quintessential expression of this culture was the tradition of the French *salon*, regular gatherings at which eminent thinkers and celebrities opened their homes to lectures and debates about contemporary politics, philosophy, theology, and the arts. Of those meetings associated with religious themes, one well-known group was hosted by the Orthodox philosopher and historian, Nicholas Berdyayev, one of many Russian intellectuals who fled to Paris after the Revolution of 1917. The playwright Gabriel Marcel headed a similar group of Christian existentialists. The *salon* that Simon frequented most often was run by the great Catholic intellectuals Jacques and Raïssa Maritain. Known as the "Cercles d'Études Thomistes" (Thomistic Study Circles), these meetings at the Maritain home in Meudon, 10 Rue de Pac in the Paris suburbs, were recognized for both the varied professions of their participants and their philosophical and political diversity. At any session, one could encounter such prominent figures as the novelist, and later Nobel laureate, François Mauriac, artists such as Marc Chagall and Julien Green, and journalists and publishers such as Emmanuel Mounier, the founder of the influential quarterly *Esprit*.

The meetings in Meudon were notable for bringing to light the deep ideological fissures that had coursed through French society at the end of the preceding century and that would continue to pit Catholic intellectuals against each other until 1945. On the one side, people like Simon were committed to finding new ways of narrowing the gap between their religious beliefs and the democratic values of the Revolution. On the other side, a host of reactionary thinkers, such as the novelist Georges Bernanos and the Catholic theologian Réginald Garrigou-Lagrange O.P., romanticized France's pre-republican glory and sought a return to monarchy. The most vocal figure among these was Charles Maurras, the leader of the Action Française, a violently anti-Semitic, proto-fascist, and royalist movement that had emerged during the Dreyfus crisis. For a time, and in a way that was more philosophical than political, Maritain himself sought to strike a balance between these two extremes. But when Pope Pius XI condemned the Action Française in 1926, Maritain promptly separated himself from the movement, enunciating his views in one of his first public commentaries on politics, *Primauté du spirituel* (published in English as "The Things That Are Not Caesar's," 1927). Yet the most significant development to come out of Meudon was not one man's principled decision to sever his ties with an extremist group but instead the choice by a significant number of the *salon's* participants and members of the Action Française to ignore the pope's words and refuse to recant their views.

This is the context in which *The Ethiopian Campaign and French Political Thought* should be understood. The reader will immediately recognize that this book is not a conventional history of the causes and consequences of Italy's assault on a distant people. Rather, for Simon, the event is a case study that allows him to formulate a moral critique. His target is the paucity of ideas and values that led a broad segment of the Catholic intelligentsia in France to shirk its responsibility to combat injustice. For one thing, Simon suggests, there was no legitimate way to defend the Ethiopian campaign in terms of the Catholic doctrine of just war. The event that began as an act of hubris and quickly reached its apogee with the use of mustard gas against thousands of combatants and civilians was a criminal act. Likewise, there was no way to defend his government's lackluster response to the crisis. Prime Minister Pierre Laval's lukewarm support of the League of Nations when it attempted to impose sanctions upon Italy was enough to cripple the international organization at a moment when it most needed to build its credibility. At the same time, the French Right's support of Mussolini's action severely damaged France's relationship with Great Britain. As a result, it became even harder for the two countries to link arms against Fascist aggression down the road.

Against this background, it is reasonable to treat one particular step taken by France's conservative elite as the centerpiece of Simon's account. On October 4, 1935, sixty-four of the country's greatest minds, including eighteen of the forty members of the Académie française came to Italy's defense. In a declaration entitled *Manifesto of French Intellectuals for the Defense of the West* (see appendix 2 in this volume), which was largely written by the essayist Henri Massis, they denounced the use of punitive measures against Italy and called upon France to declare its neutrality in the affair, lest a much more destructive conflict be unleashed on the continent. Simon had reason to disagree with this argument since he believed that France's national interests were best served by engagement. But when we consider this document today, some seven decades after it was written, we can easily understand why he was enraged by the fact that many of France's leading intellectuals had attached their names to it. The tone and character of the manifesto bear all of the markings of a class of privileged individuals whose feelings of cultural and intellectual superiority have deprived them of their capacity to make responsible ethical judgments. So haughty is its wording, in fact, that the declaration's supporters do not limit themselves to endorsing a particular policy. From the start, they subscribe to the position that their "very vocation" has imposed upon them the obligation to come to Italy's aid. In response to the supposed follies of lesser minds, they boast, "those who have consecrated their labors to intellectual concerns owe it to themselves to make their voices heard in the defense of the human spirit."

For Simon, writing in 1935, these were hardly small claims. At a time of moral and political uncertainty throughout Europe, the signers of the *Manifesto* were setting themselves up to be the defenders of everything good about the human personality. Making matters even more difficult, many of these self-proclaimed intellectuals were people who had once numbered among Simon's interlocutors and teachers, including his employer at the Institut Catholique de Paris (Catholic University of Paris), Cardinal Alfred Baudrillart. Hence, one does not need to read between the lines to see why Simon considered their statement to be reprehensible. In the *Manifesto*, the "defense of the West" that the supporters have in mind turns out to be nothing more than a rationalization of the well-worn features of European colonialism. Ethiopia, too, was a signatory to the Covenant of the League of Nations. Yet, as the *Manifesto* portrays the country, it is just "an amalgam of uncivilized tribes." Thus, the signers argue, to put obstacles in Italy's way would not only deprive it of the same right that other Western powers had exercised to express "their vitality." It would also prevent "a civilizing conquest of one of the most backward countries in the world (where Christianity itself has had no effect)."

Once again, this kind of thinking crystallized France's division into warring camps. Just as the Dreyfus Affair had done twenty-nine years earlier, this "strange orgy of vile passions," as Simon put it a few years later, demonstrated that all of the wise words, learning, and cultivated minds of French culture were not enough for France to respond to injustice with one voice. That they were taking this stand over an intervention outside of the continent was not nearly as inconsequential as it may have seemed to some observers. Italy's incursion was the first instance of a supposedly "preemptive invasion" by a European power. It represented a critical juncture in a series of events that led to the outbreak of a second world war. Would this unfathomable scenario have been different if France's elite had condemned rather than defended Italy's action? Years later, Simon told his son, Anthony O. Simon, that if there had been "one hundred politicians of integrity in France," his country might have escaped the devastation to come. In a later book, *The Road to Vichy*, written five years after the event (see appendix 1 in this volume), Simon offered several reasons for making such a judgment. Despite its shortcomings, the League of Nations had made some laudable accomplishments in the preceding years, successfully soliciting Russia's membership in 1934, heading off a conflict between Yugoslavia and Hungary, and maintaining peace in the Saarland in early 1935. Moreover, popular support for the organization was growing among the traditionally isolationist English people. Accordingly, Simon reasoned, had the French intelligentsia shown more interest in the League's survival and persuaded Britain to become more involved in continental affairs, the prospects for a viable system of collective assistance in Europe would have been considerably enhanced.

Simon was too generous in suggesting that even an ideal constellation of factors such as this one would have been sufficient to prevent the crippling disorganization and demoralization of Europe's democratic governments in the face of

Fascism. For example, the civil war in Spain would break out less than a year after Mussolini's action. But to concentrate solely on this issue would be to miss an important note in Simon's analysis that we can apply to the making of foreign policy in our own time. Just as it must have been tempting for historians in the mid-1930s to reduce the Ethiopian campaign to considerations of *Realpolitik*, the story of America's engagements in the 2000s will be equally incomplete if it is limited to the study of grand strategy. The way one state treats another, as well as the perspectives that its citizens are encouraged to have of their counterparts, can serve as valuable lenses for examining a people's commitment to certain core ideals and values. In the first decade of the twenty-first century, the expansion of international terrorism and the advent of two major wars have repeatedly tested the ability of America's leaders to abide by the moral standards that have distinguished their country in the past. Arguably, they have not been consistently up to the task. Nonetheless, the occasion of this book's release, Simon's last work to be translated into English, reminds us that the opportunity to think politically and act morally will always be available.

—A. JAMES MCADAMS
Nanovic Institute for European Studies
University of Notre Dame

ACKNOWLEDGMENTS

It is with great pleasure that I thank Gus A. and Helen Zuehlke for their continuous support of this and other Yves R. Simon Institute projects with grants from their Appleton, Wisconsin, Family Foundation. The Strake Foundation of Houston, Texas, made this project initially feasible by funding Robert Royal's translation of this work. I am indebted also to Ralph Nelson of the University of Windsor in Canada and Bernard Doering from the University of Notre Dame, who kindly translated the historical documents contained in the appendices.

The original Sheed & Ward copyright of Yves R. Simon, *The Road to Vichy, 1918–1938*, in 1942, renewed in 1970, was reverted to the Yves R. Simon Institute, which authorized the reprinting of a section of that work.

Finally, I am very grateful to Charles Van Hof, acquisitions editor at the University of Notre Dame Press, for accepting this book and Mary Katherine Lehman for her meticulous copyediting of the manuscript. They were more than enthusiastic, encouraging, and responsible for making this book a really good one. The experience was very rewarding.

—Anthony O. Simon
Yves R. Simon Institute

TRANSLATOR'S PREFACE

Ever since the creation of philosophy in ancient Greece, philosophers have had a reputation for being generally impractical and unreliable in ordinary matters. The great early philosopher Thales, according to a well-known story, allegedly fell into a hole because he was paying so much attention to contemplating the stars that he did not watch where he was going. Thales had the last laugh when he used his knowledge of meteorology to predict a large bumper crop of olives, and made a killing by monopolizing all the olive presses before the harvest came in. Philosophers, the point of the story seems to be, could make money and be practical; they just choose not to be because other things interest them more. Still, the image of the philosopher as a dreamer continues, and most philosophers who have turned their attention to practical matters, especially politics, have not shown themselves to be anywhere near as capable as Thales.

Yves Simon is a notable modern exception to the rule. Simon was beyond all doubt one of the truly great philosophical minds of the twentieth century. Among his many books it would be enough to look at *The Great Dialogue of Nature and Space, The Tradition of Natural Law, A General Theory of Authority*, and *Philosophy of Democratic Government* to be convinced of that fact. Simon was not the type of philosopher who elaborated theories and then demanded the world conform to them. He saw it as a moral task to understand human reality, and he looked upon the disorders visible throughout the West in the twentieth century not only as political, but more importantly, *philosophical* matter to be examined. If one or more countries make political errors, the remedy may be found via the normal mechanisms of politics. When countries set off on evil pathways because of philosophical errors or vicious ideologies, then normal politics is not enough. We have to think through the principles behind the situation both to fix the immediate problem and to prevent it from growing into an even larger threat.

In this philosophical analysis of contemporary politics, Simon was one of a very rare breed. The present work, the last of all his vast output to be translated into English, reveals just how rare such wisdom and justice about social affairs is among us. Today, the Italian invasion of Ethiopia and the European politics that led to it are quite obscure, even to most historians. Simon makes clear from the outset that there are certain issues at stake in the question of justice for Ethiopia that bulk as large for European political morality as the Dreyfus case did for France. Were the other colonial powers, particularly England and France, being hypocritical in condemning Italy? Did Ethiopia's membership in the League of Nations override all other considerations and demand a collective response? Were supporters and opponents of Fascist

Italy speaking urgent truths or spouting partisan slogans? Answering those and other questions requires a careful attention to fact and a prudent application of principle.

Philosophers typically fail in one of two ways when they look at concrete political situations. Usually, they do not understand that political solutions have to take into account the full set of political circumstances. Learning about and properly weighing those circumstances is hard work and requires a deep understanding of human beings and events that philosophers—typically more at home amidst abstract concepts—rarely possess. Simon shows a rich appreciation for the inescapable nature of politics. For instance, he does not think that a nation pursuing its interests is by that very fact doing something illegitimate. On the contrary, he says, we should expect nations to pursue their own interests as a matter of course. But there are different forms of national interests and different ways of pursuing them that respect the rights of other nations as well as the common needs of the international community. As a result, interests and ideals are not the terms Simon chooses as bases for judgment. He invokes the much more useful terms *illegitimate* and *legitimate* as norms for action.

Simon displays here another rare virtue in a philosopher. He does not bend the reality of politics to fit some preconceived theory but allows his theories and judgments to be informed by reality, thereby making both better because more faithful to the truth. As he puts it in a poignant and self-revealing passage in the present work:

> Realist morality demands, when confronted with every new situation, a new effort at analysis, adapted to all the particularities of the situation, the effort of an intelligence always free, always available, ready to receive everything

that the unrepeatable historical moment presents by way
of unforeseen novelty.

This is quite clearly not a Machiavellian argument in favor
of doing whatever the situation dictates. This moment of
appreciating the full reality of the situation is only a first
step, a necessary discipline before proper moral categories
can be applied: "In the perspectives of a realist philosophy,
the moralist's task consists, quite humbly, in putting oneself
in the presence of human reality to discover in that reality
some lines of perfectibility, some definite tendencies toward
a fullness always imperfectly achieved."

Because of his depth of analysis, Simon is able to show
why the relatively obscure events leading up to the Italian
invasion of Ethiopia in the 1930s had larger implications for
Europe and the world. At the same time he practices a rare
clarity about the various imperfect forces, he reminds us in
a typically pungent phrase: "if law could only be defended
by utterly spotless figures, it would never find defenders in
human societies." Recognizing this fact blunts the force of
many deliberate *ad hominem* attacks against persons and
groups and enables us to see what partial good or bad may
exist in each of them. In politics, we may often tolerate one
evil in order to avoid a worse one. Yet Simon is right that
this does not absolve us of the responsibility to reject the
evil we tolerate. As the Gospel story of the wheat and the
tares suggests, we may not always be able to uproot the latter without destroying the former, so we have to practice
patience until the final harvest.

Many people in the twentieth century thought they were
pursuing pure justice and ended up producing pure horrors. Ever the good philosopher, Simon reminds us that
even when we are about to do good actions we must beware

because "an action, just in principle, may become criminal because of circumstances." It is this sort of sophistications that enables him to be fair toward the Italians, the Ethiopians, the British, and in the very same way, to see the complex mixtures of good and bad motives among the various French factions. At the same time, his appreciation of complexities never paralyzes his overall movement of thought. He wants to know about the Italian invasion, "Is This War Just?" and closes with a profound reflection on when international institutions are or are not instruments of natural law and justice.

A word about the style of this essay. Simon can be incisive, indeed a sharp writer, when he wants to be. For example, it is not rare to come upon remarks such as this: "It is unfortunate that diplomatic habits force statesmen to clothe their aims in idealist garb; this practice contributes to the appearance of a number of foolish questions." There are also passages in the present work in which he deliberately risks a certain ruggedness and stiffness in order to spell out as clearly as possible what is at stake. A translator has the obligation to let his author make local stylistic decisions and to render these as faithfully as possible. That principle has governed various choices in the translation that appears here in the hope that the English version of this text will at least give the reader a sense for the great and original spirit behind it.

—ROBERT ROYAL
Faith & Reason Institute
Washington, D.C.

INTRODUCTION

AFTER SEVERAL MONTHS OF UNREST AMONG HIS supporters, Captain Dreyfus's guilt represented, in the eyes of national factions in conflict, no more than a secondary question.[1] France was profoundly split into supporters and adversaries of Captain Alfred Dreyfus. Whether Dreyfus was innocent or guilty, each of the two parties remained unchanged and hardened their positions. Why was it necessary for it to be thus? No one maintains that any human tribunal is infallible; that a court martial ascribed a document to one officer that was the work of another officer is an accident that does not present anything particularly unexpected, and that, in principle, dishonors no one. But quite quickly, immense historical forces coalesced around the judicial *pro* and *con*, and instead of a debate between a public minister and a lawyer, there was an existential combat in which we saw the clash of the highest regulating values of political life; a combat of spirits incarnated in powerful social formations.

Such warfare is without mercy, each of the belligerents being internally carried away by a twofold dynamic, irresistible when conjoined, of metaphysics and history. Dreyfusism was simultaneously a certain conception of justice and the will to live of groups that joined hands with such a conception of justice; anti-Dreyfusism was simultaneously a certain conception of the necessities of political life and the will to live of groups that joined hands with such a conception of the necessities of political life; both the one and the other had its god and defended a hearth; a simple scuffle between private covetousness would never have reached the dimensions of the Dreyfus revolution. Each party multiplied errors and faults, and perhaps it should be said that, in this affair, there was only one innocent person, namely Captain Dreyfus himself.

It has already been noted many times that the situation of the French nation, faced with the Italo-Ethiopian conflict, strangely recalls the Dreyfus period. In those days, ladies of the house used to beg their guests not to speak about the Dreyfus Affair; today their daughters would do well to avoid organizing a meeting between Mussolini's followers and believers in the League of Nations. France, internally divided over so many questions, is, in addition, cut in two by the expedition that a foreign state is carrying out in a distant country. Shall we say that these are merely simple differences of opinion about the way to assure what is the common goal of all French men and women, namely the general peace and France's security? Differences of opinion that bring about such a release of passions are not superficial, but deep; here, as in the time of the Dreyfus Affair, we are witnesses to a conflict of two *spirits*, of two conceptions of justice, political life, and the future of humanity. And just as at the time of the Dreyfus Affair, it is quite possible that neither of these two spirits is rooted in principles sufficiently resistant to and free from error.

The present essay is the work of a philosopher who has hardly published, until now, anything but metaphysical works.[2] It is not meant to be a historical work, or to make an original contribution to establishing the facts; *the reactions of French political opinion* constitute the object of this study. The relevance of events and governmental actions will not be re-called, or eventually judged, except as *the objects of political evaluations offered by French opinion.* This perspective seems to me to correspond fully to the philosopher's vocation and not to exceed his competence. If it is true that certain basic choices, involving the values without which life is not worth living, are implied in the positions taken by French political thought with respect to the Italo-Ethiopian conflict, it is not without interest to isolate the philosophical meaning of such choices; if it is true that the division dominant in France with respect to the Italian effort represents the conflict of large ideas incarnated in grand historical forces, it is not idle to undertake the philosophical elucidation of these ideas.

Chapter One

FROM BEFORE THE
WAR TO THE
STRESA CONFERENCE

WHAT ATTITUDES PREVALENT IN FRANCE BEFORE THE war toward the Italian nation were considered as a political formation? When I was a child, I was taught that Napoleon III committed two particularly grievous faults: he allowed German unification to occur, and he created Italian unity. The nation that owed its existence, it was said, to the intervention of the French armies, had ranged itself alongside Germany in that Triple Alliance which no one doubted would someday have to enter into conflict with France.[1] The purely defensive nature of Italy's adhesion to the Triple Alliance was ignored. The progress of the Italian navy was viewed with concern. People also spoke about the Italian threat to Tunisia. And for all that, there were French men and women who wanted it. Resentment against Italy's ingratitude was all the more keen because France was angry with itself for having forgotten, in a quixotic burst when Bonapartists joined with democrats, that ingratitude is the common practice of states.

Scorn was added to resentment. This doubtless entailed some contradictions, but public opinion did not look at it that closely. We detested Italy because its alliance with Germany forbade us, in case of a Franco-German war, to concentrate all our forces on our eastern and northeastern borders; but at the same time, we declared that the Italians were poor soldiers, a territorial army would suffice to protect the border in the Alps. We also scorned the Italians, and this was completely ignoble, because of their poverty. I remember a caricature in which bandits threatened some people who happen to be passing by: "we are Italians," they say; "we couldn't have fallen on worse," answer the bandits.

The Great War arrived; the French were quick to learn the comforting news of Italy's neutrality. Now it was a matter of getting Italy to intervene against the Central Empires. Latin brotherhood became a familiar theme in our press and *Italia irredenta* became another Alsace-Lorraine.[2] In the spring of 1915 Italy declared war on Austria-Hungary.

For the largest part of French opinion, Italy's participation in the world war is summed up in the name of Caporetto (24 October 1917).[3] Nothing has been lost from memory of the impression produced in France by that Italian defeat followed by a disorderly retreat, massive surrenders, numerous desertions. The need to dispatch several French divisions in utter haste from the other side of the Alps to contribute to the stabilization of the Italian front exacerbated the resentment and scorn of which we have just spoken. The Italian nation's straightening itself out after its defeat, the Italian victories in the final months of the campaign, did not erase the impression produced by the 1917 disaster; during the deliberations that led to the peace treaties, the memory of Caporetto caused an unfavorable prejudice toward the Italian claims: for a large number of French people, the nation whose breakdown had so gravely imperiled the Entente's cause could only hold a disadvantaged position in the division of the spoils.

We can only judge that state of mind as entirely unreasonable. Why not do justice to the Italian victories that followed Caporetto? Is there any nation that does not count in its military history some resounding disaster? After the Great War, the only interesting thing was the establishment of a durable peace. But this primacy of peace could only be safeguarded at the price of a deep rejection of all the passions generating conflicts. In reflecting on such events, we better understand that political virtue presupposes the qualities that define the man of good will. To establish peace, those directing the Entente needed an unusual degree of justice, together with the lucidity that has as its proper condition the perfect disciplining of lower appetites.

Were the peace treaties unjust to Italy? The importance of its urban acquisitions has been rightly emphasized. But it seems that the colonial clauses in the 1915 accords only met with insufficient satisfaction. Article 13 of the Treaty of London[+] was formulated in the following terms: "In case of an extension of French and British colonial possessions in Africa at the expense of Germany, France and Great Britain recognize, in principle, Italy's right to request certain compensations for itself in the form of an extension of possessions in Eritrea, in the land of the Somalis, in Libya, and in the bordering colonial districts of the French and British colonies." Note the prudence of the wording: *in principle . . . certain compensations*; the texts relating to the European territories promised to Italy were also precise. A historian, however, could write on the eve of the peace treaties about the pledges of the London accords that Italy would be "enlarged outside of Europe with vast and productive territories."[5] The same historian reports several years later that in executing Article 13 of the Treaty of London, the accord of 12 September 1919 had conceded to Italy "the elimination of the two re-entrant angles situated to the south of Tripolitania, one between El Baeka, near Rhat."[6] The "vast and productive territories" were reduced to little, and the later ceding of Jubaland by Great Britain (1924) did not notably modify the situation. Legal arguments were not lacking: One might emphasize that the treaty only entailed a commitment in principle, without specifying the dimensions of the territories in question; that France and Great Britain had not enlarged their African possessions since the former German colonies had not been incorporated into their colonial domain, but simply placed under their mandate by the League of Nations. The first argument seems to us to arise from a legal literalism that might be suspected of bad faith; the second seems to us no more decisive: though it is true that a mandate is not a possession and entails fewer advantages, France and Great Britain seem to have judged, however, that a mandate was a good thing to take; the division of the German colonies took place without conferring complete sovereignty on its beneficiaries; because of that, we believe that, in the spirit of the Treaty of London, Italy ought to have received a substantial compensation. (Whether it was a good thing that Germany was deprived of its colonies is another question.)

After the peace treaties, Italy regarded itself as harmed and resentment arose. Liberal institutions quickly collapsed, and in the autumn of 1922 the Italian Fascist era began.

Since then, French opinion toward Italy has been divided. A vast party of rabid enemies of Fascism formed: communists, socialists, radicals, Christian Democrats (in part), and Freemasons. These partisans would often assert, with sincerity in the majority of cases, that their quarrel is with Fascism, not Italy, but their position prevents them from showing themselves as favorable to Italy while that country remains Fascist. On the other side, the majority of people on the right, the nationalist and conservative parties, the most important segment of the capitalist bourgeoisie, have come to a feeling of recognition and admiration for Fascism, which would resist the harshest tests. These tests, certainly, would be harsh. The champions of liberal capitalism would not be able to avoid hearing it said that there existed an economic system in Italy that would harm their businesses, were it instituted in France; the patriots would not be able to ignore that the new Italy put itself in opposition to France, as an irreconcilable enemy of her Yugoslavian friends; in the course of the summer of 1927 no journalist denounced more vehemently than Charles Maurras the threat Italy posed on our border in the Alps and our Mediterranean coasts.

The pro-Fascist passion did not let itself weaken all the same. The French friends of Fascism did not forget that Mussolini has destroyed Italian communism, and proscribed Freemasonry; French nationalism, by virtue of its very idea, could only consider with sympathy the nationalism of a neighbor, even when it threatened and insulted France. I remember that after the bombing of Corfu, a nationalist writer of great authority wrote in order to show the happy consequences of the occupation of the Ruhr, that without the example of

Raymond Poincaré, Mussolini perhaps would not have dared launch his "lightning strike." Remember that the bombing of Corfu, carried out without a declaration of war and outside of all legal forms, or even the appearance thereof, was paid for by the death of twenty-three Armenian refugees, encamped in a fortress. And when in the spring of 1934 consultations in Venice brought Mussolini and Hitler together, many French not much earlier opposed to a Franco-German rapprochement, would say in their hearts: better a rapprochement with Hitler than a break with Mussolini.

At that date, many minds were prepared for a political rapprochement of France and Italy. Henry de Jouvenel's conciliatory mission was widely supported by public opinion. Rapprochement with Soviet Russia was also underway and the moment again came to honor the grand old principle "autonomy in foreign policy"; part of the left slackened its hostility to Fascist Italy. The governmental press allied itself with the pro-Fascist press to celebrate Franco-Italian friendship.

Several weeks after the interview in Venice, Chancellor Engelbert Dollfuss fell to the bullets of the Austrian National Socialists. German complicity was suspected; it was presumed that the crime was only the prelude to action against Austrian independence. Almost at the same time as the news of the assassination, we learned that Mussolini, confronting the guilty parties "near or far," concentrated troops on the Brenner Pass. The putsch had no sequel. The idea spread in France that Mussolini had preserved the peace. For the pro-Fascists, it was more than was asked of him; for a considerable segment of anti-Fascist opinion, it was enough to justify broad detente. The Franco-Italian accords of January 1935 and the formation of a French-Anglo-Italian front at the Conference of Stresa (April 1935) played to a highly favorable reception in the circles otherwise strongly divided on questions of internal policy.[7]

Several months earlier, the most astute observers already knew that something serious was happening in East Africa. Italy was suspected of preparing an expedition against a member state of the League of Nations. It was feared that the French government did not see itself as obliged, by the letter of the Covenant of Nations, to take part against Italy. In this way, the Franco-Italian agreement, obtained with such difficulty, would be compromised; the Stresa front, so valuable a guarantee against the eventuality of German action in Austria, would be broken; and all this to defend the independence of an African nation about which evil rumors circulated.

Chapter Two

WHAT DO WE CARE ABOUT ETHIOPIA?

WHAT DO WE CARE ABOUT ETHIOPIA! THIS exclamation, which has become familiar to many French people, is not a simple confession of incompetence; it is a positive declaration of indifference, implying some principled positions: a refusal to be interested in the fate of a foreign and distant people; indifference to respect for treaties; indifference to the long-term interests of France.

In 1921 collections were taken in university departments for the starving Russians; some comrades, and not the poorest, refused any charity, alleging that the Russians were too far away. We had learned in the catechism, however, that our neighbor means all human beings, and even if it implies a preference in favor of those nearest to us, it forbids exclusion. I notice more enthusiasm for the Italian Air Force than pity for its victims. We have forgotten the Gotha heavy bombers over Paris. Are the French farther from the Ethiopians than the Swedes and Americans?

So much for charity toward people. But this is not merely affecting some suffering people, as if it were an earthquake or flood. The existence of a nation is at stake: the affair interests all those who love their own country. Will we say that Ethiopia is not a nation, but "an amalgam of uncivilized tribes," as the *Manifesto for the Defense of the West*[1] expresses it? Let us just observe that an amalgam that for so many centuries resists so many causes for disintegration possesses a consistency that several undeniable national formations might envy. Several years ago one of the signatories of the *Manifesto*, then a professor in one of the great Parisian schools, told his students: "It is not patriotism that divides people, it is humanitarianism; patriotism draws them closer; I understand that the foreigner loves his country just as I understand that you love your mother, because I love mine." We have no explanation for humanitarianism; but it is a noble truth, this capacity of patriotism to promote friendship among people by virtue of the resemblance that exists among the patriots of all countries. The resemblance is the cause of friendship; but in what sense and under what conditions? Sometimes two people are similar in that they are both participating at the same time in one and the same perfection, and that similarity in its fullness gives birth to friendship; sometimes two people are similar in that one covets what the other possesses, and that similarity, wrongly so called, of want and fullness causes hate rather than love; thus two peoples are similar and detest one another when one covets the other's riches. There is a patriotism of covetousness and revenge that divides humans; there is a patriotism of fullness that brings them together.

Friendship founded on similarity in fullness can produce wonderful effects—it achieves a fusion of love for the nearest bandits in Marseille. We cannot love our own country so well unless we are also able to love all countries. The fact that two peoples are similar in that both possess the very great good of political independence and national dignity creates between them a community of feeling as beneficial to the common good of each nation as to peace among nations; and if war rages all the same, it will be less fierce and ignoble, which is already something. In the course of the Great War, we noted some traits of mutual esteem, of respect—why not say of friendship?—between the belligerents. "We the other soldiers," Marshal Ferdinand Foch wrote to Field Marshal Paul von Hindenburg right before his death; the British accorded great honors to the remains of the most formidable German aviators. Similar traits, which are noticed today because they are rare, were common in a still recent past. Enemy honored enemy, maintained with him a portion of friendship because he recognized his likeness in him, not only as a man, but also as a citizen and soldier, as a servant of a patriotism similar to his own.

A patriotism of covetousness has existed in every age. It has always coexisted with a patriotism of fullness. And hatreds among nations are also of every time; the respective dimensions of the two patriotisms have varied, what has been lost by one is gained by the other. I love my country for what it is, for what it has of perfection; at the same time, I want for it what it lacks: it is normal for the two feelings to go together, but their volume or intensity vary in inverse proportions. According to whether the preponderance belongs to the patriotism of fullness or the patriotism of covetousness, patriotism can be a factor for either unity or division. The perfecting of national hatreds, which is one of the most considerable facts in the moral history of the present age, seems to us to correspond to a newly acquired preponderance of the patriotism of covetousness over the patriotism of fullness, a preponderance that coincides with inflamed economic interests. Our patriotism can remain indifferent to Ethiopia if it consists solely of covetousness, if it is reduced to a low and always dangerous form of patriotism.[2] But the French who felt the national sorrows of Belgium and Great Britain; those who could understand and feel the element of national greatness that Fascist Italy or Hitler's Germany contain, despite many dark or sinister dimensions, those people cannot say, *"what do we care about Ethiopia?"*

To be uninterested in Ethiopia is, in addition, to proclaim oneself indifferent to respect for treaties; though it is true that few people are in a position to gauge the precise legal position of the Italian-Ethiopian question, no Frenchman is unaware that the Italian enterprise implies the violation of several international commitments. But we will return to this point.

Finally, to be uninterested in Ethiopia is it to sell cheap considerable and perhaps vital certain French interests? The least that can be said is that we are not sure. It would have been fitting to be sure of this before declaring that the affair does not concern us.

It seems that we have not understood the deep reasons that suggest today, with growing probability, the idea of the indivisibility of peace. Recent experience attests, however, that conflicts in the modern world have a tendency to become general, even without the assistance of the League of Nations. What a shame that the League of Nations did not exist in 1914! Perhaps general war would have been avoided. If war had been avoided, those detractors of international institutions would have declared that the credit belonged to the power of the Entente; if war had occurred, they would have accused the League of Nations of having caused a general conflict that would have been simple to limit to a settling of accounts between the Dual Monarchy and Serbian bandits. But the League of Nations did not exist, and the detractors of international institutions have not had the consolation, in the midst of universal suffering, to incriminate the "Protestant and Masonic Babel."

The casualness with which those who are called the representatives par excellence of French patriotism have treated the long-term interests of France in this Italian-Ethiopian affair is quite striking. A lightness comparable to that of Napoleon III. Should we have been surprised? "It is we socialists," a young militant told me, "who are obliged to be patriots." I did not share his astonishment. Patriotism has become a partisan merchandise like any other. Patriotism is retailed here as socialism, or whatever else, is retailed elsewhere. Depending on circumstances, the good of the nation will be served sometimes by one party and sometimes by another. Naturally, allowing for the reality of as many exceptions as one may wish.

Chapter Three

THE
ANTI-FASCIST
CRUSADE

TO THE PARTISANSHIP OF INDIFFERENCE WITH respect to the fate of Ethiopia another sort of partisanship quickly replied: blaming the Fascist government. The opportunity was too beautiful. Since the advent of the Fascist regime, the revolutionary parties of every country repeated that Fascism meant war, and at the same time oppression and destitution. It takes an uncommon elevation of soul to resist the delight of having been right. Just as the nationalists would always register displeasure for the League of Nations, so too the anti-Fascists, or at least the most resolute among them, looked forward to exploiting every error or every fault committed by the hated regime. The time had come to make an end of it; grappling with the difficulties of its African expedition, placed outside the law by the international community, hit by economic sanctions and perhaps military ones, the Fascist force would quickly fail; and that would be the great event so much awaited, the vindication of the exiled. In their inmost hearts, the right of Ethiopia only played a secondary role. And the passion was so great that we might have feared that it represented a danger to the peace.

The simple suspicion that the force of international institutions could be put to use in an anti-Fascist crusade introduced considerable perturbation into the posing of international problems. Those sanctions that the legal texts present as the sword of international justice, how would they not have been tagged with a presumption of partiality if it had been proven that some of their advocates had resolved to use them for their partisan passions? Some French feared in good faith that France should not be drawn into an ideological war. The pro-Fascist press would exploit that fear with consummate art.

We will not examine the reasons why an important segment of French and world opinion considered that nothing was more urgent than overturning the Fascist regime. Not that we fear such an examination: but this is not the place to pursue it. We do not ask here about the value of the means by which the Fascist regime was established and is maintained; whether it represents a defensive reaction by bourgeois capitalism or whether, on the contrary, it represents, as was said of National Socialism, a kind of Bolshevism; whether it ruined Italy or whether it has pointed the way to prosperity. Though we are not unaware of any of these questions, we refrain from putting them here. We will look at the Fascist regime as a historical given provided with all the prerogatives that the Christian conscience and that philosophy recognize in the established order.

Alongside the anti-Fascist passion, we must mention, among the factors that have vexed the fair posing of the problem, a certain spirit of systematic hostility to every attempt at colonization. Even if it were only a spirit of distrust, it would be abundantly justified by the many and serious abuses to which colonization has given rise, in peace as in war, in earlier or more recent colonial efforts. But it is always a disastrous sophistry to misunderstand the legitimacy of a principle because of the abuses that accompany its application, whatever may be the frequency and volume of those abuses. Since it is legitimate in law under strict conditions, no one can say *a priori* that the attempt at colonization would in fact be illegitimate in some particular case: we only have to be sure that the particular case safeguards the conditions of legitimacy.

Some people will point out that anti-Fascist passion and anti-colonial passion, whatever their intrinsic quality, can, by a happy accident, serve justice, if it has been established that the colonial action engaged in by the Fascist state is contrary to law; the situation would be analogous to that of a work of benevolence that takes advantage of a generosity inspired by impure motives. But such accidental successes are always precarious; the intrinsic force of motives always ends up getting the upper hand. Works of justice and charity that are not willed for the sake of justice and charity always end by betraying justice and charity. The essential motives for voluntary actions are more powerful than chance, and threaten actions rooted in chance with invalidity. To take the great moral question raised by the Italo-Ethiopian War to its moral essence: Is this war just? This is what, before all else, must be recognized.

Chapter Four

BUT IS
THIS WAR
JUST?

AS WE HAVE RECALLED, THE ITALIAN MILITARY action involves the violation of several treaties; if we abstract from actions prior to Ethiopia's entry into the League of Nations, three treaties still forbid Italian troops to enter the Mareb: the Covenant of the League of Nations, the 1928 Italo-Ethiopian Treaty, and the Kellogg-Briand Pact, signed in Paris in 1928. This is more than is necessary to create a presumption of injustice.

Some people will think that the term *presumption of injustice* is too weak, that the violation of a treaty is enough in itself and independent of all circumstances to render a war clearly criminal. True morality, in our opinion, does not entail such rigidity, and its concrete decisions do not allow themselves to be discovered at so little cost. Just as there exist limit situations when insurrection against the established power is legitimate, so there are limit situations, rare though we may think them, when a treaty arrived at in good and due form ceases to be obligatory.[1] It will be necessary therefore to take the trouble, before declaring a policy involving the failure to observe a treaty as unjust, to be sure that we are not dealing with one of the limit situations. Realist morality demands, when confronted with every new situation, a new effort at analysis, adapted to all the particularities of the situation, an effort of an intelligence always free, always available, ready to receive everything that the unrepeatable historical moment presents by way of unforeseen novelty. Such an attitude is in no way to be confused with empiricism or opportunism; the true men of action are simultaneously very careful about doctrine, principles, constant rules, and very careful to maintain in their minds that open space where, in the concrete, decisions that are highly detailed arise.

What, then, is that *absolute morality* that is deemed incompatible with the necessities of political action? Thierry Maulnier reproaches the *Manifesto*[2] by some Catholic writers of employing, against civilization, "the weapon of absolute morality"; Julien Benda wants the absolute moral positions to be energetically recalled; both declare that temporal life has some demands that do not accord with those of absolute morality. The universe of human action thus would admit of a polar opposition in which it is easy to recognize a Manichean essence; what might be gained through absolute morality would be lost by trying to make temporal bodies live by it, and vice versa.

We believe we can recognize in this phantasmagoria an *idealist* conception of morality. In the sense that the word *idealism* bears in modern philosophy, metaphysics is idealist to the extent that it considers the objects of our knowledge as simple products or simple moments of mental activity. For a realist philosophy, perfect cognition is the faithful reiteration in the mind of things that are the measure of the mind; for an idealist philosophy, perfect cognition is the wholly conscious construction of an entirely transparent universe. In the perspectives of a realist philosophy, the moralist's task consists, quite humbly, in putting oneself in the presence of human reality to discover in that reality some lines of perfectibility, some definite tendencies toward a fullness always imperfectly achieved. The essential tendencies of human nature, the lines of perfectibility resulting from man's specific nature, are expressed by the body of natural laws, by natural right; born from the investigation of essential realities, the formulas of natural right need to be further developed through formulas relative to contingent circumstances where the essential tendencies operate. For the living reality that needs to be guided to its perfection is a compound of necessity and contingency, of essence and history, of nature and adventure. The immediately regulatory judgment of the act is only fully moral when it takes account of all the circumstances affecting, in whatever way, the play of the essential tendencies of the human reality and the application of natural laws. Among these circumstances there may be some that are unsettling, in such a way that the concrete moral judgment would take the form of an exception to a law, by virtue of the demands of a higher law. In the classic example, the general law: *one must return what has been entrusted* may be suspended by a higher law when the thing entrusted is a weapon, and if the one who has entrusted it to another is a criminal or madman. Similarly, we understand that an unsettling circumstance may come to suspend, in an exceptional instance, the law requiring the carrying out of treaties. Thus, the moral rule, oriented toward the absolute of the final end, is at the same time always relative to the highly variable complex of the action that it is supposed to regulate. Under these conditions, the notion of absolute morality appears to be an ambiguity without real use: true morality scoffs at that concept of absolute morality.

The notion of the moral absolute is an idealist notion. Just as it tends to make the object into a product of mental activity, idealism tends to make of normative judgment a pure emanation from practical reason—pure, which is to say, independent of being. To the concept of the good, which means nothing more than the real, or being, in as much as it is desirable, in as much as it is apt to present itself before a will, idealism substitutes the concept of value, which is intended to express the fiction of a goodness emptied of reality. The morality that results from these fundamental positions is truly an absolute morality, detached from life and destined to enter into conflict with it. It is too easy, in truth, to oppose the demands of life to the prescriptions of morality when we have begun by breaking the essential relationship that morality maintains with life.

Realist morality, because it admits the possibility of complications that may suspend the application of the law by virtue of a higher law forbids us to hold a war as manifestly unjust for the sole reason that it involves a failure to observe treaties. But the contingency that suspends the application of the law does not abolish the law; the possibility of a complication that may suspend the law will not occur except in the smallest number of cases; law, having necessity in its favor, will also have the great number of instances in its favor, and whoever discards it will be presumed to be in the wrong, until what he has done offers proof of his right. Whoever refuses to return what has been entrusted to him is presumed dishonest: it is up to him to prove that a higher law opposes the return of what was entrusted. To deny that *evidence* of injustice accompanies all failure to observe the law is simply to recognize the potential for mitigating complications; to deny that a *presumption* of injustice accompanies, even to the best informed, every failure to observe the law, is to flout the law itself.

Now that is the fault of which some French have made themselves guilty when they have given their sympathy to the Italian effort in a spirit of indifference to the violation of treaties. Even supposing that extraordinary circumstances have legitimized the failure to observe the treaties that guarantee the Ethiopian Empire's political independence and integrity, the attitude of indifference to the law that says treaties should be respected is no less an outrage to justice. That attitude of indifference defines the legal system as mere scraps of paper.

Chapter Five

ETHIOPIA'S
FOREIGN
RELATIONS

ETHIOPIA'S FOREIGN RELATIONS ARE DETERMINED
in their essentials by three sets of interests: French, British,
and Italian.[1] In France's colonial economy, Djibouti plays a
twofold role: it is a port of transit on the route to Indochina
and Madagascar, and it is a commercial agency in relation
with the center of Ethiopia by means of the Addis Ababa
railway. As we know, this railroad was built by a French
company at the cost of great difficulties and innumerable
human lives (an indigenous worker per rail section, it is said,
and a European per kilometer). It appears that in no period
did French policy try to enlarge the highly limited territory

of the colony: its territorial ambitions found their satisfaction elsewhere. French claims on the Ethiopian power concerned the security of Djibouti and the ease of commercial transactions. Under these conditions, ordinary diplomatic relations sufficed to handle the difficulties of the neighborhood.

Three British possessions have common borders with Ethiopia: British Somalia, Kenya, and Anglo-Egypt Sudan. We know the importance of this last possession in the general economy of the Empire. Physical geography establishes some vital connections between Sudan and Ethiopia: the waters of the Blue Nile, which assure the fecundity of both Sudan and Ethiopia, come from the Abyssinian mountain range; British policy looked to constructing, on several occasions, a regulating dam in the region of Lake Tsana; it could only view with extreme disquietude a foreign power's establishing control over the waters of the Blue Nile. In addition, the projected construction of a railway line linking the Cape to Cairo provided for crossing Ethiopian territory. In the years that followed the Great War, British policy openly aimed at establishing domination over the western part of Ethiopia; in 1922 the British press carried out a campaign against Ethiopia using many of the same arguments the Italian press used in 1935. Ethiopian independence was being threatened, but it was preserved by Ethiopia's membership in the League of Nations.

The whole set of Italian interests presents an entirely different picture. While Great Britain and France possess immense colonial empires, Italy only has colonies of small extent and poor yield; the worst of the bargain from the colonial point of view among the great European nations (except Germany) is to experience, owing to rapid population growth, a lack of land and poverty of the soil, the most pressing reason for expansion. When Italy entered into competition with colonial nations, the carving up of the desirable territories had already been achieved, at least to all intents and purposes. If there remained on earth any territories still available for the creation of an Italian empire, it was in Ethiopia and nowhere else. This is one of the great, dominant facts that should never be forgotten. We might say that owing to the nature of things, by virtue of arguments constantly arising about human liberty through an irrevocable set of historical facts, every Italian effort in Ethiopia, whether military or not, would have the character of an effort at conquest. Faced with an Italian effort in Ethiopia, whoever wanted to maintain that it was a matter of a defensive operation had to furnish proof; historical probability favored the opposite interpretation. The Ethiopians understood that, and that is why the building of an Italian railway on their territory appeared to them something to be feared for entirely different reasons than the building of the French railway.

In 1870 an Italian shipping company was installed at Assab (Eritrea); Massawa was occupied in 1875; Assab was declared an Italian colony in 1882; the Italian advance into Eritrea would be halted from 1887 to 1889 following defeats at Dogali and Saganeiti; in the course of those two years, Francesco Crispi established his government's protectorate over Somalia by means of treaties with local chiefs.

In 1889, shortly after the death of Negus Johannes,[2] the Italians gained a foothold on the Abyssinian plateau (occupying Asmara and Keren). They gave their support to Menelik against his competitors; they signed the Treaty of Ucciali with him (2 May 1889); this treaty specified the borders of the colony of Eritrea and established, according to the Italian version of the text, a kind of protectorate over the Ethiopian Empire. There was a difference in wording between the Italian and Amharic versions sufficient to conceal,

in Menelik's view, the clause drawing up the Italian protectorate. In February of 1893, Menelik rejected the Treaty
of Ucciali; the first Ethiopian campaign, which began with
victories, ended with the Adowa catastrophe (March 1896).
The Treaty of Addis Ababa (October 1896) annulled the
Treaty of Ucciali and recognized the full independence of
the Ethiopian state.

For a while anyway, Italy apparently abandoned its imperial projects; it worked to develop Eritrea and Somalia; the
agreements it reached with the Ethiopian government or
with the bordering powers aimed at the consolidation of its
possessions and the development of their commercial relations. Toward 1910 the idea of colonial expansion came back
into favor through the nationalist group, *Idea Nazionale*.
Popular enthusiasm forced Minister Giovanni Giolitti to
declare an ill-prepared war on Turkey (29 September 1911);
a year later the Turkish government, attacked by Balkan allies, abandoned the region around Tripoli.

The Great War intervened, followed by considerable
metropolitan enlargements for Italy and colonial setbacks.
Would Italy return to its colonial aims in Ethiopia? In 1923
Italy did not resist Ethiopia's entry into the League of Nations. In 1924 Italy received the Regent Tafari in friendship.
Then in 1928 the Italians signed a treaty of friendship and
arbitration[3] with him that seemed to mark a definitive aban-
donment of an attempt at military conquest. Not that Italy
abandoned the possibilities for expansion Ethiopia offered,
or that Ethiopia would have offered Italy had the Ethiopians
been better disposed toward Italy; but the means foreseen
were not those of a violent action.

On 5 December 1934, the Walwal incident occurred, followed by the Afdub incident on 29 January 1935. The whole
world quickly understood that something had changed.

Around the same period, a French official, the administrator Bernard, and the small force that he commanded, were victims of Ethiopian irregulars (18 January 1935); the affair was settled without further damage, without particular difficulties. We immediately understood that Italian-Ethiopian incidents were not subject to the ordinary settlement. On 17 February 1935, the first battalions of Black Shirts embarked for Eritrea; the same day, a communiqué from the Fascist Grand Council led us to foresee a widespread action. The situation was clear: Italy was returning to its intention to create an empire in East Africa.

Chapter Six

THE
MAD DOG

FROM THAT TIME ON, WE SAW THE MULTIPLICATION of Italian accusations against Ethiopia, which were abundantly reported by the French press. The accusations were of two kinds: some related to the internal situation in Ethiopia and intended to present the campaign then in preparation as a war for civilization. Others related to Ethiopia's foreign policy and were intended to convince public opinion that it was a matter of legitimate defense. We will look at the first set of grievances a little later; here we will consider the second set.

Italian memoirs report on numerous border incidents, of attacks of all kinds against Italian figures, of frequent failures to respect treaties. It is quite possible that some of these facts were exaggerated, others were unverifiable. But from our point of view this has little importance. It suffices that the events reported were perfectly believable and no one questioned them. Let us situate ourselves within the hypothesis most favorable to the Italians' contentions. Let us admit that the alleged facts are all well established; let us even admit, in spite of appearances, that all the wrongs were on one side. A question remains which renders suspect the whole Italian argument: were Italy's reasons for grievances aggravated after 1928 to the point of justifying *in themselves* such a change in attitude on Italy's part? In 1928 Italy signed a treaty of friendship and arbitration;[1] after the beginning of 1935, it openly wanted war. Were the reasons for the change primarily on the Ethiopian side, or indeed were they primarily on the Italian side? Did the dog go mad, or was it that the man discovered some reason to have done with it?

On the Ethiopian side, all that seems certain is that the resistance to Italian penetration did not lessen from 1928 to 1935, but that resistance is perhaps only the fact of a nation determined to preserve its independence. The preponderant reasons for the change in the Italian attitude must be sought on Italy's side. To be convinced of this, it suffices to refer to the propositions of Mussolini and his press: "We will have work for fifty years in Ethiopia." Italy's leaders, to the extent that they were concerned to justify their African effort in the eyes of world opinion, which they did not hesitate to defy if need be, invoked legitimate defense and just cause. You would have to be blind not to see that the will to conquer had priority among them over the chances for defense. That will to conquer, slumbering after Adowa, reawakened: that is the essential change that explains the transformations in the Italian attitude with respect to Ethiopia. The condition of the dog had surely changed little, but the man decided to have done with it; he therefore declared that the dog had gone mad and if that did not meet with sufficient credence, after all it matters little: the intended action will be carried out nonetheless.

Under these conditions, are we faced with a war of conquest, pure and simple? Pope Pius XI declared in a speech that the fact that a majority of the French press has failed to point out the seriousness of a war "which is nothing but a conquest" is something so unjust and horrible that one does not wish to contemplate the possibility. In expressing himself this way, the pope, following the approach of a moralist, judged that the understanding of typical cases is the first condition for understanding mixed cases. I cannot, for example, judge the legitimacy of an investment which simultaneously has the nature of a contract for a loan and the nature of a social contract unless I have previously determined the typical kinds of loan contracts and social contracts. In the concrete form of events, moral types rarely present themselves in a pure state. The historical event is a complex of several types: it is at the same time, for example, a war of conquest and a war of defense. The serious business is to decipher the type that occupies the dominant place and plays the decisive role in the complexities under consideration. Has there ever been a war of pure conquest between states having common borders? The existence of common borders between two states almost always entails problems that justify certain defensive measures. None of the actions that have made France master of North Africa has been a pure war of conquest. It was necessary to conquer Algiers to secure Mediterranean traffic, then Algeria for the security of Algiers, then Tunisia, the Sahara, and Morocco for the security of Algeria; who would contest, for all that, that the occupation of North Africa by French forces was primarily an operation of conquest? Napoleon was led to conquer all Europe through wars, each of which could invoke motives quite different than a desire for conquest, none of which was a war of pure conquest.

Italy never gave up its projects for expansion into East Africa; but we have seen that it seems indeed to have given up an effort at military conquest in 1928. Why did its military designs regain force in 1935, a year when the general conjunction of events appeared as unfavorable as they could possibly be? The moment was specially chosen. Economic crisis, great financial difficulties, widespread disquiet, the German threat in Central Europe: a variety of factors that should have strongly suggested a postponement of the planned expedition. Many people affirmed that Mussolini was laboring under a delusion about the difficulties of a war in Ethiopia. Did he think that it was only a matter, as some French journalists foolishly wrote, of a *motorized touring* party, of a courageous and glorious *weekend*? It is impossible to believe that the Italian leader was more unaware of the conditions for his enterprise than were the most poorly informed French. The immense and ruinous deployment of men and materiel that was carried out prior to the opening of the campaign does not seem to correspond with the illusion of an easy victory. "I am betting everything on everything," Mussolini himself declared in July 1935 to Henri de Kérillis. That was the pressing reason why the Italian government would go and risk its future in Ethiopia at the very moment when the Italian nation, like most of the European powers, found itself confronting a crisis that threatened to lead it to bet, in other words, everything on everything, but on other battlefields. This question of the chosen moment is of supreme importance for understanding the whole affair. Italy's internal situation provides the only plausible answer. A policy of ruinous expenses and of passionate enthusiasm made this situation untenable. A financial catastrophe was menacing; what would its political consequences be? The regime could not do without an external victory. It had failed in the Balkans, failed in its attempts at an agreement with Germany, given up Tunisia and its initial irredentist pretensions in French territory. Nothing remained but Ethiopia.

If this is correct, and the best testimony obliges us to believe so, many historical precedents will help us to understand what has happened. Was it not in similar circumstances that Napoleon III, to the delight of Bismarck, invited the French enthusiasts and the "super-ready" to depart for Berlin?

"We are lost," an Austrian said prior to the Great War, "nothing but a successful war can get us out of this." On 24 October 1918, Count Ottokar Czernin noted that the Dual Monarchy had reached the end of its life. The rescue attempt had cost around twelve million human lives.

Chapter Seven

ETHIOPIA'S INTERNAL SITUATION

EVERYONE KNOWS THAT THE VAST TERRITORIES subjected to the suzerainty of the Negus contain immense natural riches that have been little developed. A better use would assure that these riches would contribute to the common good of humanity. It would also add to the prosperity of the Italian nation, so disagreeably lacking in raw materials. These are the things that appear completely desirable. It has to be recalled once more—regrettably, we are obliged to do so—that wars over oil, phosphates, diamonds, or opium have never passed, in the eyes of Christian conscience and natural law, for just wars. A more difficult question concerns the possibilities of European inhabitation of Ethiopia: it indeed seems that these possibilities are very small, especially since the habitable regions desired by Europeans are already densely populated.

On Ethiopia's political and social condition, the essentials, insofar as they involve the moral problem posed by the Italian enterprise, seem to have already been discussed at length. Do the Italian memoirs and the reports in our pro-Fascist press contain exaggerations? That appears to be the case, but is hard to verify. What is certain is that Ethiopia's internal situation presents a very somber picture to the eyes of the most sympathetic observers. The central power is weak, intrigues and civil wars are frequent; security of persons, especially travelers, is only mildly bothered about; mores recalling the most frightful barbarism persist in certain regions; the justice system is cruel, education barely developed; the rude state of technologies, ignorance, and poverty contribute to very poor sanitary conditions; slavery, in various forms, has spread everywhere; slave raiders continue despite energetic attempts to eliminate them. None of this is in doubt, and there is enough here for us to put the question of the legitimacy of a foreign intervention; we reject in effect the liberal principle of non-intervention: theology and common sense agree in recognizing the possibility of internal situations so inhuman that they justify intervention by foreign powers, potentially through force of arms. Such situations represent few cases, doubtless quite rare ones, but their existence must be admitted. Is Ethiopia one of these limited cases?

We note first that it is always easy to move people by describing, even in strictly non-exaggerated terms, what is most unhappy about a country, without saying anything about the favorable sides of the situation. The story of Ethiopian atrocities, accompanied by photographic documentation, was able to convince many that the Italian enterprise, all questions of oil aside, represented a magnificent humanitarian crusade: the image of a tank shooting out death is easier to bear than that of a mutilated child. Everyone lives daily in forgetfulness that the human condition—though in differing degrees—involves frightening things. Our souls are too weak to bear the image of horror: that is why we remain ignorant of the horror present in our midst, and content ourselves with satisfying our sense of virtue by decrying the horror that rages among distant tribes, demanding that it end. Just imagine what the picture of contemporary France might be if we only kept aspects of such dark visions, even without exaggeration! Though the Negus is often helpless in the face of his large feudal subordinates, isn't the government of the French Republic at every moment held in check by less open, but no less undisciplined powers? These powers occasionally commit acts of civil war; but what is even more serious is that they contribute to increasing the chances of an international war that would kill more French in a month than the feudal disputes in Ethiopia would kill Ethiopians in a century. Destitution and pathological death rates? Just think about our numberless unemployed, about unhealthy living conditions where so large a proportion of our urban population live in moral and physical decay. Leprosy may rage in Ethiopia, but tuberculosis kills 100,000 French each year, of whom a great number could be saved if public funds were used to build healthy dwellings and sanatoriums: rather than being used to produce war materiel. (I do not wish to say that our military expenditures, in the current state of international relations, are not necessary. I only want to recall that, even in peacetime, they kill people, we too often forget.) What about slavery? We no longer have slaves or serfs—at least on our own national territory—but several million French, subjected to proletarian conditions, shoulder a freedom sometime heavier than slavery. Finally, as to the abuses of the justice system, certain reports about our own civil and military jails have been no less sensational in their time than the stories that come to us today from Ethiopia.

I am not unaware, in writing these pages, that certain readers will have me say that Ethiopia's internal situation is no worse than that in a nation abundantly endowed with the benefits of Western civilization. You can never stop partisan people from accusing those they regard as opponents of whatever stupidities appear to be most useful for the cause. What I wish to say here is that part of the destitution and crime observable within Ethiopia's primitive system, which is used to provide arguments to justify foreign intervention, could equally be observed in one of the longest civilized countries in Europe. This observation applies exclusively to the reasons brought forward for foreign intervention and does not question the merits of our civilization. There is in every human society a portion of evil that civilization does not abolish; that element of evil must be deducted from the liabilities of the nation whose internal situation poses the question of a just intervention: that is all.

Second, it has to be asked, what will be the real possibilities for a European conqueror who will have assumed the function of bringing civilization to a backward people, strongly ensconced in the double citadel of its mountains and age-old customs? Are the conquerors magicians? The British regime never ended the famines and epidemics in India. The Negus has shown himself powerless up to now to stop the slave raiders on the outlying areas of his empire; will the Italians, installed as masters in Addis Ababa, achieve more? Let us remember that these raiders have as one of their main aims the stimulation of the slave trade in Arabia; to go from

Ethiopia to Arabia you must pass through Eritrea, French Somalia, British Somalia, or Italian Somalia; since the trafficking continues to occur, it is clear that the colonizing nations are unable to keep watch over the coasts where they are sovereign; nothing allows us to think that any one among them will succeed in establishing within a short time more effective control over the pathways followed by these sinister caravans. And if we have to look forward to a long-term effort, the benefits of foreign intervention become doubtful. The Negus Haile Selassie strove for twenty-five years to achieve total suppression of slavery; there are powerful reasons to think that the Italian forces would not reach the desired result in a significantly shorter time. And the same is true of the majority of the other reforms needed.

Third, we have to note that the means of reform used by a European conqueror are necessarily burdensome. The resistance that the Negus's action met with will not be less opposed to the actions of a foreign power. To overcome them, violence will be inevitable. We will not take any more pictures of hands cut off, but there may be more heads cut off, which no one will have permission to photograph. If we are dealing with institutional abuses such as slavery, we should be worried that the reform undertaken by a European power does not replace them with even worse abuses. Forced labor such as is widespread in the colonies of equatorial Africa or Ethiopian slavery—which is worse? It is not obvious that it is Ethiopian slavery. Supposing that Italian colonization avoids replacing slavery with forced labor, we may look with disfavor on the creation, especially the rapid creation, of a free proletariat in Ethiopia.

Finally, we must consider that European civilization, introduced into Ethiopia by colonial conquest, will simultaneously introduce all of Europe's bad sides as well as its benefits. Midwives are already lacking for childbirth among the Senegalese. But during the Great War, bullets, shells, and poison gas were not lacking for the Senegalese. I do not want to say that a colonizing nation has the right, under certain conditions, doubtless severe ones, to invite its protégés to come to its defense but we must allow that in this, from the indigenous point of view, we have one of the burdensome sides of colonization. If the Italians had not been beaten at the Battle of Adowa, there is no telling how many Ethiopians might have been killed at the Piave or the Isonzo fighting for the Italians.

When we take the trouble to stop and think about these things, wars of colonization considered as a beneficent intervention lose a large part of their allure. For a violent military intervention by a foreign power to be justified by a country's internal situation, it is not enough, let us note, that it be undertaken to bring about an amelioration of that internal situation. It must also be the case that the proposed amelioration is substantial enough so that it greatly exceeds the immense evils implicit in war.

No one has disputed that Ethiopia's internal situation justifies intervention; but the only intervention that promises a net gain in good results over the inevitable devastation would be collective intervention, the only type that can be peaceful because it is the only type that can accept Ethiopian patriotism. An intervention of this kind would doubtless have better served Italy's true interests, which would not seek to engage in a murderous and ruinous war, full of incalculable diplomatic consequences. But worries over domestic politics and prestige have come to be all mixed up together.

For the largest part of French opinion, the war for civilization was quickly, and definitively, a game won. Testimonies of sympathy multiplied. Scruples, if there were any, were well stifled by the idea that the former colonial nations had already done many similar things: in lending to the Italian undertaking the character of a humanitarian enterprise, it was our bad conscience that we were trying to clear. The especially violent behavior of the Italian armies only caused a passing embarrassment, quickly dissipated through established passions.

"We have the undeniable right," wrote *Il Regime Fascista* on 29 November 1935, "of recourse to all means, licit or illicit, to destroy the barbarians: an eye for an eye, a tooth for a tooth.

"Let's start by dropping hundreds and hundreds of pounds of poison gas bombs in the valleys where the enemy camps, and if necessary, tons. This is the only way to receive with proper dignity the Swedish officers who announced they were going to the front lines, at the head of the army of the Negus.

"If they dare to protest in Geneva, or if England raises objections, we will answer them with Cambronne's saying."[1] Some weeks later, the Swedish ambulance from Dolo was destroyed. The name of the *Lusitania* was repeated throughout the world. But French testimonies of sympathy for the civilizing war continued to abound. Ought we be surprised? During the war of the Rif Mountains, Charles Maurras had conducted a savage campaign for the use of poison gas; he recognized that the practice would require tearing up a piece of paper that bore France's signature. The French authorities resisted his exhortations and the gas was never used against the Riffains. But if Maurras's campaign produced no victims among the populations of the Rif Mountains [Morocco], we see today that it has produced innumerable victims among French souls. It goes without saying that if we name Charles Maurras rather than someone else, it is not because of some special partisanship against him personally, but simply because he is the most logical and in every way the greatest representative of a whole set of groups that think like him about the moral basis of political problems.

Chapter Eight

THE COVENANT
OF THE LEAGUE
OF NATIONS

DURING THE PEACE CONFERENCE, THE WORD SPREAD
to Addis Ababa that the French government was prepared to
cede Djibouti to Italy.[1] The Regent, Prince Ras Tafari (Haile
Selassie) believed that there was a threat to Ethiopian independence and proposed, afterwards, to seek his country's
entrance into the League of Nations; the proposal obtained
the support of the French government, but the French, fac-
ing the hostility of Great Britain, had to give up pursuit of
implementing the proposal.

In 1922 the British press took up a campaign against
Ethiopia, which we have described. In September of the same

year, when the League of Nations put the question of slavery on its work agenda, the New Zealand delegate submitted an act of accusation against the Ethiopian government; at the Council meeting, which took place in June 1923, the French representative expressed the wish that the Ethiopian government be heard: the Italian delegate refused. Then, some French friends counseled the Regent Tafari to address a request for admission to the secretariat of the League of Nations. The petition, dated 19 August 1923, was supported by the French government, whose president was Raymond Poincaré who was represented in Geneva by Henry de Jouvenel. Let us try to untangle what were the most important characteristics in the debate that ensued.

1. It was France that led the charge, and to its delegates are owed the merit and responsibility for Ethiopia's entry into the League of Nations. Those who have stated, in regard to the Italo-Ethiopian conflict, that the League of Nations is only an instrument of the Foreign Office have forgotten, or have pretended to forget, that Ethiopia was admitted to the League of Nations at the price of the victory of French influence over British influence.

2. The opposition was led by Great Britain; it was vehement, obstinate, and made use of arguments similar to those that Italy developed in 1935 to obtain Ethiopia's exclusion.

3. Italy's attitude remained reserved for a while; it does not seem right to say, as has often been done, that Ethiopia was admitted at Geneva through the request of France *and* Italy; the Italian delegate ultimately gave in to de Jouvenel's arguments, but from the totality of his remarks it seems rather that he had favored delaying tactics.

4. Did Ethiopia fulfill the legally required conditions for its entry into the League of Nations? The reports presented on this subject lead to a conclusion in the affirmative; they

leave, however, the impression of reservations and hesitations on several points of great importance: the authority of the central government, the determination of borders, fidelity to international agreements, arms and munitions trafficking, and the struggle against slavery.

5. De Jouvenel, in accord with the policy that France followed after its settlement on the Somali coast, conducted himself as a resolute partisan for Ethiopian independence, and an open friend of Ethiopia; he trusted in Prince Tafari's desire for reform; he affirmed that Ethiopia's entry into the League of Nations was the surest way to achieve the speedy abolition of the abuses and disorders in the Empire's current situation.

6. In entering the League of Nations, Ethiopia had undertaken some reform commitments; and the League of Nations, for its part, had committed itself to that labor of reform. It does not appear that, on either side, these commitments were fully observed. Materiel impossibilities, negligence, bad faith? Let us merely recall that in 1934, eleven years after Ethiopia's entry into the League of Nations, no effective determination was reached whether Walwal, located according to the theoretical border inside Ethiopia and more than a hundred kilometers away from Italian territories, belonged to Ethiopia or Italian Somalia.

Was Ethiopia's admission into the League of Nations, unanimously declared by the Assembly on 28 September 1923 a mistake? This is the view not only of all the cynics, but also of several loyal and fervent advocates of international law. It would be outside our present purposes to take sides on this question. By way of a reminder of principles, we will only say here that if participation in the rights of a member of the League of Nations supposes a minimum of political maturity, it is no less true that one of the functions of international society is to protect weaker nations and to facilitate, according to de Jouvenel's way of thinking, the progress of developing nations. But whatever we make of the opportunity offered by an indisputable decision, that decision remained. And Ethiopia, whether rightly or wrongly having become a member of the League of Nations, should have enjoyed the benefits of what had been decided; without this, international law would be subject to chance and would offer security to no one; Laval's government understood that, despite its strong desire not to displease Italy.

At the beginning of December 1934, an Anglo-Ethiopian Commission charged with making an inventory of the grazing lands in Ogaden arrived at Walwal; an Italian military post had occupied the place since 1930. When a dispute arose between the Italian commandant and the head of the Ethiopian force, the English withdrew; no neutral witnessed the battle that took place on 5 December and the following days between the Italian and Ethiopian forces. Each of the two parties held the other as obviously and exclusively responsible. The League of Nations was immediately informed of the affair by the Ethiopian government. Events quickly developed along several lines.

1. The first related to the arbitration procedure envisioned in the 1928 Italo-Ethiopian Treaty. Italy, believing that the question was all too clear, resisted the activation of that procedure for a while. The Ethiopian government stated in advance that it would accept any decision emerging from arbitration. The arbitration commission was not formed until May 1935; the judges, who were four in number, did not arrive at any conclusion. A fifth judge joined them at the beginning of August, but the Council of the League of Nations, deciding in favor of the Italian government's demands, forbade the commission to examine the question of

borders: it was then necessary to rule on the responsibilities for a conflict between territorial troops and foreign troops without knowing which were the territorials and which the foreigners. By the time the commission concluded on 3 September that it was impossible to demarcate clearly the responsibility of either of the two parties, its existence had almost been forgotten.

2. The efforts at conciliation by France and Great Britain made up a second line of developments. Negotiations among the three powers adjacent to Ethiopia began in April. Then on 24 June, Anthony Eden had a conversation with Mussolini. The British minister proposed intervening with the Negus in order to obtain a set of territorial and economic concessions favoring Italy. Great Britain offered Ethiopia, by way of compensation, an outlet at the port of Zeila (British Somalia). Mussolini rejected these proposals. On 3 August the Council of the League of Nations decided that the powers who had signed the 1906 tripartite agreement should consult together as soon as possible with a view toward working out a plan for a comprehensive solution. The tripartite conference was held in Paris, 16–18 August; the French and British governments submitted a project to the Italian government for collective intervention in Ethiopia: France, Great Britain, and Italy, acting in accord with the League of Nations or by virtue of its mandate, would lend help to the Ethiopian government in order to assure the reform of the Empire; Italy would thus obtain security of its colonial frontiers and possibilities for economic expansion; its interests would be the object of privileged treatment; some territorial concessions could be envisaged. Mussolini entirely rejected all this.

3. The Council of the League of Nations had thus delayed as long as possible direct intervention by the international authority created by the Covenant; more than eight

months after the initial incident, the League of Nations had still done nothing more than encourage and coordinate attempts at arbitration and reconciliation, resorting to classic diplomatic practices.[2] Rightly or wrongly, it remained in the background up until the total checkmate of all its efforts. When the Council of the League of Nations met on 4 November to examine the whole problem, Baron Pompeo Aloisi read an indictment of Ethiopia from which might be gleaned the terms of a declaration of war.

Another effort at reconciliation was tried, however; a five-member committee established a program for collective intervention that seemed of a nature to give Italy the best guarantees of security and the best chances for economic expansion; some Franco-British proposals for territorial concessions were added to this plan; the Negus accepted the Committee of Five's proposals, even though they might lend themselves to the establishment of a protectorate in everything but the name; it was also known that he was prepared to abandon vast territories in the southern portion of his empire. On 22 September, the Italian delegate communicated his government's rejection of the terms to the president of the Committee.

Meanwhile, from 17 February on, the Italian forces were massing in Eritrea and Somalia; the Eritrean troops crossed the border on 3 October; on 7 October the Council of the League of Nations unanimously recognized that "Italy had resorted to war, contrary to the commitments in article 12 of the Covenant." On 10 October, fifty countries approved the Council's decision to apply the sanctions provided for in the Covenant against the aggressor.

Chapter Nine

BRITISH

POLICY

IT IS UNFORTUNATE THAT DIPLOMATIC HABITS FORCE statesmen to clothe their aims in idealist garb; this practice contributes to the appearance of a number of foolish questions. Many people have gravely asked whether Great Britain was pursuing its own interests in this affair, and they believe that a yes or no answer would shed a decisive light on the international situation. What should we think, truly, about a government that would leave out of its preoccupations the interests of the nation that it governs? We will put the question in entirely different terms; we are seeking the motives for the British intervention, without asking whether they deserve the rather useless qualification of being interested or idealist. The distinction between legitimate motives, in accord with the right of each and the common good of international society, and illegitimate motives, seems to us much more certain and fruitful than the parliamentary distinction between interest and ideal.

It is a matter of course that in a case of such great historical importance, an unlimited number of motives enter into play, and interpenetrate one another. It is not even certain that it is possible to designate a main motive to which all the others are subordinated. What seems possible to us is to draw out the whole set of dominant motives.

We have earlier alluded to the undertakings tending to assure Great Britain's dominance over Western Ethiopia. It is beyond question that British policy, having recently decided to exercise its own control over the waters of the Blue Nile, looked upon the arrival of an Italian force in the Lake Tsana region with great uneasiness. That anxiety was insufficient, we believe, to explain by itself the intervention with which we are familiar; it was a second-order factor operating in concert with other factors. We would attribute a similar character to worries relative to the security of the route to the Indies. The Italian arrival in Eritrea did not elicit any British protest, and the Eritrean colony, for a half-century, in no way compromised freedom to pursue the imperial path; the occupation of the Ethiopian hinterland doubtless brought about a considerable strengthening of the Italian power on the shores of the Red Sea, but why would that power be hostile? Everything depended, in truth, on the intentions that Great Britain ascribed to the Italian government. Difficulties that would have been easily resolved given confidence, took on a tragic bearing when they arose in a context that was itself tragic. If there had only been the question of Lake Tsana and of the route to the Indies, the British intervention would have had a hard time not being unjust; it would only have been a way to oppose the necessary expansion of the Italian nation.

But it was an entirely different matter; the British statesmen had seen a great imperial formation emerging from Tripoli to Mogadishu; Marshal Italo Balbo, sent to Libya upon his return from Chicago, did not refrain from action; he had organized a powerful army whose use could not be understood except as a threat to Egypt. Threatened in the west by Libya's troops, Egypt ran the risk of also being threatened in the southeast on the day that the Italians subjugated Ethiopia and integrated its army; it had also been hit with propaganda that could quickly lead to revolutionary acts. At the same time, the development of Italian aviation abolished the defensive value of the port of Malta; Great Britain's supremacy in the Mediterranean could be compromised in the near future. And the bellicose declarations took their normal course, which was highly antipathetic to the British people. All this constituted an alarming set of circumstances.

British diplomats and journalists thus expressed these alarms; soon, and this was perhaps the decisive event, Italy reacted with a campaign of mad provocations. If the celebrated interview [*Times* (London), 1 August 1935] with Henri de Kérillis is accurate, Mussolini is supposed to have said to his interviewer that a statesman must let himself be guided by instinct rather than by perusing history books. Instinct, perhaps, does not know that you do not provoke British power without consequences; but history bears witness to that. Concentration of the British fleet in the Mediterranean was the response of insulted imperial pride: a dangerous operation, without question, but inevitable for anyone who was not ignorant of the historical constants in British politics. What would it have come to if the League of Nations did not exist, if the two Mediterranean imperialisms, the old and the new, had confronted one another head to head?

But the Covenant of Nations provided Great Britain with the guarantees that it thought necessary. British policy would be total faithfulness to the Covenant, which did not prevent it from taking part in the efforts at conciliation which were animated by the French government. The colonial conflict that Italy spoke about, the conflict between Italian and British influences in East Africa and the Mediterranean would become, through Great Britain's resolve, resting on international commitments, an event without historical precedent: the conflict of one of the members of the international community with the whole international community.

Two years earlier, the most faithful supporters of an organized international society allowed themselves to be overcome by discouragement. Created in the first place to establish peace in Europe, the League of Nations showed itself incapable of stopping the spread of the most fearsome symptoms; the arms race began again and many minds, more and more, resigned themselves to the prospect of a war a hundred times worse than the one in 1914. The checkmate of the League of Nations in confronting the Sino-Japanese conflict, the secession by Japan, then by Germany, seemed to portend the progressive dissolution of the Geneva institution. Many French found that just fine: we had lived in the clouds for fifteen years, real life was finally about to start again.

Several events followed, however, of a nature to breathe new life into the organism that was believed to be near death; first, was the membership of Soviet Russia, then the successful interventions of the League of Nations in the Hungarian-

Yugoslavian dispute, and in the Saarland affair. Numerous French were waiting to receive their mobilization letters around the fateful date of 11 January 1935; things occurred in complete calm; the intervention by the League of Nations had avoided a highly feared risk of conflict. The League of Nations had opportunely shown a remnant of life at the very moment when Europe had most need of it. When it took charge of the Italo-Ethiopian conflict, the League of Nations had just achieved results that *might* mark the beginning of a period of correction. Everything depended on the new test: if it wound up successful, great hopes would be justified; if in failure, that failure would be the last. Both the supporters and the opponents of the League of Nations understood this with equal lucidity. The game would be decisive, and it would be played out on both sides with ferocious resolve. The case for the League of Nations would be supported above all by the British nation; the case for the opponents would be represented above all by the French Right.

The desire to save the League of Nations and to affirm its authority seems to have played a first-order role in determining British conduct. To say that Great Britain, needing assurances against Italy's African and Mediterranean ambitions, employed the instrument that the Covenant provided is to say far too little: the truth is that Great Britain had to seize, with passion, upon the first opportunity to serve the League of Nations. Because it was Britain that had felt itself threatened by the developments in continental political relations; because Britain had continental political relations; because Britain had committed itself, after long and regrettable hesitations, to the collective security party; because Britain had understood that the most powerful nations ran the risk of becoming, perhaps quite soon, *someone's Ethiopia*, it had to think of international law as the very law of its own national safety. Let us not lose sight of the meaning of the Peace Ballot and that unity of the British people, moved by an extraordinary emotional energy, in the adherence to a policy of peace based on the obligations of the Covenant.[1]

Great Britain's role in this affair could not help but seem loathsome; "it's that we," wrote Jean Guéhenno, "have four or five Ethiopias on our back." The spectacle of a nation provided with an immense colonial empire, acquired by God knows what means, intervening in the name of the law against an overpopulated nation that cruelly lacked colonial outlets, inevitably would have to take on the appearance of an enormous hypocrisy. Our actions follow us and there was nothing to do to save appearances, which an indelible past had decidedly compromised. But Ethiopia was a member of the League of Nations and it was indeed necessary that someone would defend the law. And if law could only be defended by utterly spotless figures, it would never find defenders in human societies. The loyalty of the powers already provided with colonial possessions, their respect for each member's rights and their faithfulness to the common good of the international League would be measured by the attitude they would adopt, in the near future, in light of the ineluctable problem of the redistribution of colonial benefits.

The British policy of observing the Covenant made the French squarely face a choice of incalculable importance: *indeed either* France would declare itself in favor of the Covenant, and its acts would follow those of Great Britain; and in that case, the institution of collective security would pass beyond the stage of written law to the stage of historical practice, and if someday France were the victim of an aggression, it could count on British help; *or indeed* France could relieve herself of the Covenant's obligations, but in that case, the institution of collective security would become a dead letter, the possibility of British neutrality in the event of an aggression directed against France would not at all be discounted. Some inveterate partisans of nationalism, known detractors of the League of Nations, understood what that option would mean for France and their patriotism was aroused; but for the majority of the French right, Great Britain's intervention was only an additional reason, and how effective, to conduct the campaign against the League of Nations. The belligerents and the party men did not like fighting on several fronts at the same time; the collusion among their adversaries facilitated their strategy; to strike with a single blow all those that were being fought against, to hate with a single hatred all those who were detested, what a precious economy of munitions and passions! Behold, thus, all those who hated the French right gathered together in one place: such occasions are rare. There were the theoreticians of international law, the pacifists, the humanitarians; there was anti-Fascist democracy and the kind of socialism that was the enemy of colonization; there was Free Masonry being fought against, to hate with a single hatred all those who were detested, that were full of resentment against Mussolini; there were the Jews, numerous among the Masons and the socialists; there was the Soviet Union, represented by Maxime Litvinov; there was Edvard Beneš and Nicolae Titulescu who did not want the Archduke Otto; there were the nationalists from all the colonized countries, full of sympathy for a country that refused to allow itself to be colonized; there was, finally, England, the competing nation, the hereditary enemy, the land of liberalism, the nation where the kings are democrats.

Chapter Ten

THE INTERVENTION

OF THE

INTELLECTUALS

AT THE BEGINNING OF AUTUMN 1935 WHEN IT WAS
certain that Italy would not avoid the application of the
sanctions provided for in the Covenant, or at least of the
more mild among them, French opinion was deeply affected
by a sharp uneasiness. The Italian government's arrogant
attitude, the challenges launched by the Italian press toward Great Britain and the League of Nations created fear
of a mad and desperate gesture by a country abrogating
the Covenant against the nations faithful to the Covenant.
What would Germany's attitude be then? The threat of a
new European war, always hanging overhead ever since

the peace treaties, impressed itself more than ever on many minds. Without question the Fascist press and its French allies liberally used the threat of war as blackmail to assure the ineffectiveness of the Covenant, but the other side of the anti-Fascist crusade, as we have already noted, sometimes gave the impression of being led by men determined to make an end, no matter what the cost, to the Mussolini regime. We know where such resolutions can lead, rooted in the absolutes of an ideology and swollen with blind resentments. It was useful to recall that the European peace ought to be maintained in any case and that the application of the Covenant had to be regarded as impossible to the extent that it risked evils disproportionate to the injustice that it sought to prevent.[1] Human societies, whether national or international, must tolerate evil when they are incapable of repressing it without causing still greater evils. But the potential duty to tolerate one evil to avoid an even worse one does not dispense us from the primary duty to refuse evil. Indeed, the refusal of any interior adherence to evil is the indispensable point of departure for every effective action in favor of the good.

Thus we can grant to the adversaries of sanctions without hidden motives that while applying sanctions might have threatened the general peace, and it was necessary to affirm before all else the absolute desire to save the general peace, should one for all that reject just sanctions in principle? In expressing ourselves this way, we do not in the least wish to assert that every sanction imposed by the League of Nations against Italy would have compromised or later risked compromising peace in Europe; we simply want to recall that an action, just in principle, may become criminal because of circumstances. The statesmen and their counselors, whether intellectuals or not, need to judge the circumstances.

Didn't the *Manifesto for the Defense of the West* propose the affirmation of a resolute desire to avoid the worst evil and to preserve peace in Europe? It was in that spirit that several of the signers approved it.[2] It would be difficult to contest that its writers, as sincere as they were in their desire for peace, made out of it something quite different than a simple peace declaration.

The title itself is already surprising. If it were only a matter of peace, why not call it by its rightful name? Peace is neither Eastern nor Western, and the Prince of Peace arose in the East. The text opens with a massive affirmation, excluding at the outset the spirit of discernment which is part of every impartial politics: "At a time when Italy is threatened with sanctions that may very well unleash a war without precedent, we, as French intellectuals, insist on declaring before the entire world that we wish to have nothing to do with these sanctions or this war."

It seems that afterward, the sanctions with which Italy was threatened were repudiated, and not solely as a potential cause of war, but also condemned in themselves. That was not long in becoming entirely clear: "They do not hesitate to declare Italy guilty and, before all the world, to point to it as the common enemy. . . ." If it was wrong to treat Italy as guilty, then Italy was innocent. The Italian undertaking was then likened, in the clearest way, to a just war, and the certainty of tone indicates with what scorn the violated agreements were held, even if they carried France's very own signature. A hurtful sentence follows, one that had great psychological success, with respect to the Ethiopian nation: ". . . under the pretext of protecting in Africa the independence of an amalgam of uncivilized tribes. . . ."

The Western humanists' apology (in appearance perfectly useless, for there is no need to be a dedicated Westerner to reject war) quickly developed, manifesting its reasons for its being, an apology for the bad conscience of the colonizing nations: "On this very notion, in which the West incarnates its ideals, its honors, its humanity, great peoples, like England, like France, have founded the most fruitful expressions of their vitality, as a justification of their work of colonization, which remains one of their most exalted. And would not these great powers be obliged immediately to abdicate their own colonial mission, if they wished, without deception, to forbid Rome from pursuing the same in those regions of Africa, in which it has a long time ago acquired incontestable rights, the accomplishment of the plans which it has honestly formulated and openly prepared?"

In those few lines quite a few things are mixed up. First, we notice that the colonizing nations avail themselves of Western humanism to justify their conquests; it affirms that the work of colonization by England and France was great and fruitful. But we are not told whether the chance to promote Western humanism is really enough to make a war of colonial conquest just; we are not told whether the happy results of colonial conquests—or rather of some of them, an important nuance missing from the text—retroactively establish the justice of those conquests; we are not told anything about all this, but the discussion proceeds as if it all goes without saying. Thus we use two implicit untruths to arrive at where we wished to arrive: *first*, that promoting a higher civilization justifies in itself a war of conquest; *second*, that a good result justifies in itself the act from which it proceeds. Are we forgetting that the Lord of contingency knows how to bend evil to the service of good and to draw wonderful results from an evil act? When some great benefit—the constitution of an ordered state, the pacification of vast territories, the proliferation of the Christian faith—results from a criminal act—an unjust war, for instance, an annexation without legitimate title, a religious persecution—there is nothing else to do than adore the Divine Goodness. The crime from which the divine governance knows how to draw out good remains a crime, and its happy consequences, which are imputable to God and not to the criminal, do not suggest that it ought to be imitated. For it is implied that the colonizing wars of England and France, whose legitimacy is summarily postulated, can be legitimately imitated in the very special conditions that Italo-Ethiopian relations offer. It is here that contempt for treaties is most decisively expressed.

It is not true that, in pursuing the application of the Covenant, England and France forbade Italy "the accomplishment of the plans . . . honestly formulated and openly prepared"; in pursuing the fulfillment of the Covenant, England and France, and forty-five other nations with them, wished to safeguard the independence of Ethiopia; now the plan for putting an end to that independence, far from being faithfully formulated, was categorically excluded by the treaties that Italy signed, and of which the other nations are guarantors. It is not true that, in opposing themselves to an unjust colonial undertaking, England and France obliged themselves to abandon "their own colonial mission"; even supposing that their colonial conquests had been entirely unjust, the colonizing nations would still have, by virtue of the *fait accompli*, a colonial mission even more pressing, a duty of assistance toward the colonized peoples even more demanding, so that the justification of the *fait accompli* would not be even more doubtful. Finally, it is not true that in pursuing the preservation of Ethiopia's independence along lines laid out in the Covenant that the nations possessing colonies were hypocritically opposed to the justifiable ambitions of young

Italy: they were only opposing *in this* an ambition contrary to law. Italy's just colonial ambitions were, we believe, misunderstood in 1919; we wish them to be fully recognized in a future conference on colonization, even if it costs our nation certain sacrifices; but the recognition of just ambitions in no way absolves us from the duty of opposing unjust ambitions.

Next, the *Manifesto* denounces the egalitarianism practiced by the League of Nations; it notes in passing the support among revolutionary forces for the British action; it insists on the wrongs of "a false juridical universalism which places on the same basis of equality the superior and the inferior, the civilized and the barbarian." Here, too, much confusion. Was it a question of whether it was good or not that Ethiopia had been admitted to the League of Nations? Opinions about this question are many, and we have noted that some determined defenders of the League of Nations regard Ethiopia's admission as a mistake. But that is not at issue today since Ethiopia, rightly or wrongly, was admitted to the League of Nations and benefits from that prior decision. Underneath the passionate claim for just hierarchy, we are afraid that we see a dark intention of substituting consideration of subjective inequalities, pure and simple, for consideration of legal rights. Some rights are equal, whatever the subjective inequality of those who bear them. Between Belgium and Germany, subjective inequality is indisputable, and we think, nonetheless, that Belgium's right to independence is no less sacred than Germany's. It would have been necessary to demonstrate that Ethiopia had lost its right to independence: the *Manifesto* thought it better to limit itself to equivocal declamations about the "mania to equalize," which had come to possess international institutions.[3]

Chapter Eleven

REFLECTIONS ON CERTAIN RESISTANCES TO THE PROGRESS OF INTERNATIONAL LAW

DID SOME FRENCH BELIEVE THAT THE LEAGUE OF Nations would never mobilize the powers of its members except in defense of our territory? We must believe so, since the plan introduced by André Tardieu at the Disarmament Conference did not cause his friends to desert him. Thus the League of Nations' attitude toward the Italo-Ethiopian conflict might cause surprise among people who were poorly informed and poorly equipped to understand the meaning of legal realities. These disillusioned souls, we believe, only played a weak role in the campaign currently underway against the League of Nations; considered in its totality, the campaign is only the chance manifestation of a spirit that has been active for fifteen years; its tone does not express shock, but, to the contrary, wild pleasure at having been right; for the majority of the opponents of the League of Nations' action in our country today, the present dangers are only a triumphant confirmation of what they have always predicted. We would like to try to understand here the reasons for this tenacious and impassioned hostility.

1. The popular opinion released right after the war in favor of a League of Nations seemed to many French to be nothing other than the continuation and repetition of pre-war pacifism. Inevitably, it shared in the discredit of that earlier movement. The totality of efforts that we are designating by the name of pre-war pacifism had contributed to the insufficiencies of our defensive preparations. All those, whoever they might be, who had advocated maintaining the peace by non-military means, all those who had opposed the increase in the time of service and expenditures on arms were held by an important segment of French opinion as primarily responsible for our defeats in 1914 and in the war itself. The breakup of the Workers' International made a great impression on very different circles. Too many French had sincerely believed that, in case of war, the international proletariat would withdraw and would respond to the mobilization order with a general strike; the opponents of socialism feared that this possibility might be realized in France, they had little hope that it would happen in Germany; the socialists, on the contrary, believed that the feelings of the German proletariat, the most powerful and most socialist of all the proletarians, would constitute a major guarantee in favor of peace. We know what happened: as soon as war was certain, the proletarian formations in each country reunited themselves to the national unity and while René Viviani

tore up *Notebook B*[1] the German socialists were voting almost unanimously for war loans. No one had believed such a radical defection was possible. The French noted in particular the defection by the German socialists and swore not to be taken in a second time. From then on it was a widespread notion in our country that military power constituted the *only* guarantee of peace and that every attempt to ensure peace through the friendly collaboration of peoples corresponded to illusions that the outbreak of war in 1914 had irrevocably revealed.

In our opinion, the behavior of the proletariat and of the socialist leaders in 1914 demonstrated above all else a failure of the notion of class: it testifies that the tendency of the proletarian class to withdraw from the rest of the nation is limited by its tendency to reincorporation in the national whole. The attempts to guarantee peace by collaboration among states had nothing, in principle, in common with an internationalism of class that implied, in the measure to which it is effective, the disintegration of divergence from political wholes. As to the policy to follow on the question of armaments (or alliances) it was entirely conditioned by the international situation: in some circumstances, an intense arms build-up is a guarantee against war, in other circumstances it might be a menace to peace. The project of the League of Nations did not imply in itself any resolution to pursue systematically whatever the circumstances, the reduction in national armaments; rather than presuppose an unrealistic disarmament the League of Nations had the task of creating a situation that would make it prudently possible to reduce military burdens.

2. We cannot emphasize enough the importance of the historical linkage between ideas about international organization and certain ideologies, which caused strong antipathy

among French conservatives and among numerous minds in no way systematically conservative. In the history of French thought, aspirations for the organization of international society were found represented in abundance among people who were, at the same time, proponents of international socialism, cosmopolitan individualism, anti-militarism tending toward anarchism, Masonic millenarianism, and many other errors. Just because the Masonic lodges ardently advocated the League of Nations, we clearly did not have to conclude, in strict logic, that the idea was to be counted among Masonic errors; but public opinion, to say nothing of informed people, cared little for strict logic; subjective coincidences spoke as eloquently as substantial connections. Furthermore, the subjective mixture of ideas led to the contamination of ideas with one another; an idea that sojourned, matured, in an impure environment, would itself be charged with impurities: this was unquestionably the case for certain regulative notions proposed for France's membership by the best known proponents of the League of Nations. To accept them as they stood was to accept, mixed together with valuable truths, errors, which were necessary to reject at any cost.

The problems stemming from this historical mixture of ideas were found in every social sector and at every point in time, and the solution that they called for was always the same: *whoever had pure intellectual instruments at his disposal should try his best to carry out the necessary work of purification.* May they never be wanting at the hour when history calls upon them, these liberators of captive truths! The problem that arises today with regard to international law arose three centuries ago with regard to the new scientific spirit; it arose with regard to the development of democracy, the development of industry, the growth of the proletariat; the question has arisen a thousand times, and every time that it has not been answered, great disasters followed.

Let us observe here that the inability to guide an idea that has arisen historically in the midst of a complex of error to the purity of truth is an indication of weakness and servitude, an index of an insufficient strengthening of the mind in truth, which is power and freedom. There are open spiritual societies whose readiness to accept anything condemns them to dissolution; there are closed spiritual societies who assure their survival by making a desert around them; there are open spiritual societies that have conquered in welcoming, and it is ever their proper life, the life of their very idea that endures and progresses by incorporating ideas conceived in another's heart. I think of the Islamic attitude—and that of the Catholic Church—when faced with medieval Aristotelianism; the faith of the Koran having been threatened by the philosophers, Islam decided not to speak of them any further, and Averroës was the last of the great Arabic philosophers. An Averroising Aristotelianism was no less perilous for Christian faith than for the faith of the Koran, but the Church desired further discussion, and after Averroës there was, in the Church herself, St. Albertus Magnus and St. Thomas Aquinas. Without minds sufficiently rooted in the truth, the Christian world—I do not speak of the teaching Church—sometimes resembles a conservative citadel of the Muslim kind, and sometimes exposes itself to liberal dissolution (modernism).

3. Another general factor of hostility toward the League of Nations derived from the seductions of force. In the dialogue of force and law, some deep inclinations dispose us toward attributing to force a sympathetic and glorious role; it is impressive how the spouse in the Song of Songs is *terribilis ut castrorum acies ordinata*: the law is merely a simple civilian.

Today so many confused things are written about law and force, which perpetuate disorder in many consciences, that it seems particularly timely to us to make an effort to elucidate these notions of force and law, and at the same time, the problem of their connections with one another.

If we go over the various accepted meanings of the term *force* as it is currently used with respect to human relations, it seems that the decisive elements in its meaning can be summarized in the following formula: force is an active causality, having as its object a person or society, and whose proper effects are of a physical nature; the person or society who uses force pursues a physical effect, or an ensemble of physical effects, as the proper means to their ends. The most typical example of the use of force is the mechanical causality exerted by one man on another: boxing, battle; a non-mechanical operation such as a strike, the organization of economic privations, refusal of credit, etc., are equally acts of force, for here, too, a certain physical effect (hunger, for example) is taken as the proper means toward an end.

Thus, force is usually the opposite of persuasion, whose proper effect is of moral nature. Between force and persuasion there exist some quite remarkable points of contact: force often generates persuasion and, in turn, persuasion, when it takes possession of human masses, gives birth to a kind of force; thus, a public opinion campaign, or even the practice of the interdict, as it was used in the Middle Ages, are undertakings of persuasion that generate force.

Among the multiple uses of the term *law*, the first in the order of intelligibility seems to be the objective usage: law, which is before everything else the just, is the action that renders to another what is due; law is before all else *the object of justice*. We use the word law, in a second place, for the *rule* of just action (the *formal* meaning of the term *law*);

finally, we call law that faculty that someone possesses to whom something is owed to assert his due (*subjective* meaning). There exists an objective natural law whose rule is the natural law; there exists an objective positive law, whose rule is of human institution: that rule is sometimes a contract agreed upon between persons or communities, sometimes a law established by a community. If we understand the term *law* in the formal sense (in the sense of the rule or measure of justice) there are then three great species of law: natural law, positive contractual law, and positive legislative law. In a complete juridical system, the contractual relations are subordinated to positive laws, which are only true laws to the extent that they themselves conform to natural laws. The inner regime of a state is in principle a complete juridical system. The regime of international relations, so long as there does not exist any international community capable of establishing laws and imposing their implementation, is an incomplete juridical system: it only admits as other rules of law the natural laws and contractual stipulations; *positive legislative law is wanting here.*

Within an organized community, furnished with a positive legislative law, force is nothing other than the instrument of a rule of law, nothing other than the instrument of the positive law in its function of effectively regulating juridical matter. In these conditions, we rarely speak of conflicts between force and law; such conflicts can only occur in entirely accidental cases. There is a conflict between force and law, within an organized political community, when public force is used in the service of an unjust law; there is a conflict between force and law when the public force is held in check by a rebel force; finally, there can be a conflict between force and law when private groups confront one another in litigations in which the law does not envision the solution (the class struggle, for example); but in the last case, we have a real lack of positive legislative law.

Let us now consider the formal juridical situation of sovereign nations still not committed to an international community. What are the character and role of force in such a situation? Must we say, as is often done, that we are dealing with a regime based on force, which should be replaced, pure and simple, with a regime of law? These very terms—regime of force and regime of law—seem confused to us, and their opposition to one another lends itself to ambiguity. We will therefore try to put the question more precisely by asking if a national force *is forbidden* in the absence of a positive international law to play the role of an instrument of a rule of law. Surely, the possibility of such a role for national force is not excluded; every time it is used to ensure the observation of a natural law or a contractual stipulation itself conforming to the natural law, national force has played the role of an instrument of the rule of law; but nothing guarantees, unless it is the virtue of a specific government, that it will play this role rather than the opposite role; nothing guarantees that it will not be checked or crushed by a rival force. The first benefit of organized communities, capable of establishing laws and imposing respect for them by collective force, is to increase immensely the chance of success for a rule of law. Is it possible to extend this inestimable benefit to international relations, to the very limits of the borders of the states? This, in a few words and stripped of all parasitic ideology, is the problem of the League of Nations.

We can only marvel that many people think the prospect for a true League of Nations, an institutional community provided with a legislative power and possessing means of constraint, is unrealizable: the possibilities of history are only definitely established once they have been verified in a completed history. We will not be further surprised that the potential problems in introducing a regime of positive legal law into international relations have been pointed out; whatever the intrinsic excellence of positive legislative law, in some circumstances, its establishment may bring with it more problems than advantages; it is possible, for example, that the suppression of the class struggle by subjecting relations between the bosses and the proletarians to positive legislative law, has not always been a beneficial reform. But the opponents of the League of Nations did not content themselves with judging the project of an institutional international community unrealizable: they *wanted* it to be unrealizable; they did not content themselves with calling attention to potential inconveniences: they wanted those inconveniences to be prohibitive. Their opposition did not hinge solely on the real possibilities of the application of a principle but bore also on the very principle of the extension of the regime of positive legislative law to international relations.

Here, we mean by the term *violence* not, as is often the case, the unjust use of force, but every use of force that lacks the character of an instrument of positive law; a just war, a just strike, a just insurrection, are in this sense acts of violence; arresting a delinquent, stopping a riot, sanctions applied by the international community to a state unfaithful to the international law are acts not of violence but of legal force. Now, it must be observed that justified violence—without speaking about what is not just—has aspects that are lacking in legal force. Justified violence, like work, has a dual end. Work first aims at the production of real wealth, and there its end is objective and primary, but secondarily it aims at the cultivation of the worker (subjective end). Justified violence aims in the first place at the application of the rule of law, and secondarily at the exaltation of the group that uses it.

This subjective function of violence has been magnificently described by Pierre-Joseph Proudhon in *La Guerre et la paix*, by Georges Sorel in *Reflections on Violence*, and by Édouard Berth in *Guerre des États ou guerre des classes*. When a social group is engaged in violent action, all members of the group are subjected to a discipline restraining egoistical aims and inferior appetites, and are spurred in lively fashion by heroic sentiments; the strike, Édouard Berth liked to say, feeds socialism just as war feeds patriotism; it is thanks to the demands of violent action that social groups receive from their members the devotion needed for their solidarity. The antagonistic violence of groups produces in many cases marvelous effects of mutual pedagogy; Hannibal educated the Romans, the Swedes educated Peter the Great. Would not proscribing violence from international relations compromise the cohesion of states and their vitality, and at the same time exhaust the most accessible springs of heroic feeling?

However that subjective end of just violence is only a secondary end; its primary end is the triumph of the rule of law, and if that primary end can be attained more surely, more constantly and at less cost by legal force, such force must unconditionally be preferred. In truth, if the apologists for violence put the subjective ends of violence on the highest plane; then they forget that, in any cause, violence is only respectable on the condition that it be just; if it is only a question of exalting heroic feeling and reinforcing group cohesion, unjust violence is worth more than just violence, and the epic of Napoleon surpasses the epic of Joan of Arc. But then we have to understand that we have no interest in justice and that such a conception of heroic war has nothing in common with the Christian conception of just war.

Furthermore, it must be asked whether modern conditions of war forbid violence to play that moralizing role that certain wars of the past were able to play. P.-J. Proudhon addresses the question; after celebrating the virtues of war in pages of extraordinary lyricism, he demonstrated in no less stunning a fashion that modern war is no longer in a position to exercise these ancient virtues. The book that opens with an apology for war ends with its condemnation. When Mussolini cites Proudhon, it is to the first part of *La Guerre et la paix* that he refers.

Proudhon's book appeared in 1861; since then, we have been abundantly edified about the moralizing aptitudes of modern warfare. The protests raised by Erich Maria Remarque's novel expressed the confusion of certain minds about indications that from now on we must look elsewhere than to war for a source of enthusiasm and devotion.[2] Universal conscription, bombing of civilian populations, the use of gas and incendiary liquids, the whipping up of mass hatreds hardly lend themselves to ennobling souls.

Chapter Twelve

7 MARCH 1936

AT THE MOMENT OF WRITING THESE LAST LINES, the Italian armies have just won important victories; thousands of men are dead; the League of Nations is trying one last effort at reconciliation; Great Britain has confirmed its resolution, in case of the failure of this effort, to pursue the strengthening of sanctions. Now suddenly the focus of universal anxiety has shifted: the Hitler government broke the Treaty of Locarno and reestablished its military power on the left bank of the Rhine; at the same time, it proposed, under certain conditions, to re-enter the League of Nations.

Any prediction now would be overbold; all Europe fears catastrophes before long; if we do not want to compromise our last chances for safety, this is more than ever the time to impose silence on our passions. In such circumstances, everything that might come to trouble our lucidity of judgment would give another chance to the most immense evils that threaten us. Silence then for the party spirit, silence for nationalist passion, for anti-Fascist passion; silence for hatred, even hatred that takes as its object indisputable criminals. All political agility will be powerless if it is not ruled by a clear-seeing and honest interior attitude.

It is with respect to a problem of interior attitude that this book has been written; it has no other end than to contribute, if it pleases God, to the rectifying of French consciences in the love of truth, justice, and peace.

APPENDIX 1

Ethiopia Revisited:
The Road to Vichy

Ed. note: This appendix presents Yves R. Simon's views on the Italo-Ethiopian War some five years (1941) after the publication of his *Ethiopia* book. The following extract, with modifications by Anthony O. Simon, is taken from Yves R. Simon, *The Road to Vichy, 1918–1938*, trans. James A. Corbett and George J. McMorrow (New York: Sheed & Ward, 1942), 105–17; rev. ed. with an introduction by John Hellman (Lanham, MD: University Press of America, 1988; reprint 1989), 105–17. In the original French edition, *La Grande crise de la République française: Observations sur la vie politique des français de 1918 à 1938*, Problèmes Actuels 4 (Montréal: Éditions de l'Arbre, 1941), see 121–35.

*   *   *

Germany was still in the early stages of her intensive rearmament when another dictator state made known to the

world its intended aggression. During the spring and summer of 1935 it became obvious that Italy was intent on con-
quering Ethiopia.

The French had many reasons to oppose this undertaking.
It was their duty to oppose it, first of all, because it was a
manifestly unjust war. The question which then confronted
the Christian conscience was this: would the teaching of the
Catholic Church on the war be taken seriously,[1] or would
it be assumed that this teaching was merely a theoretical
and academic matter, useful for exercising the argumenta-
tive minds of theology students, but irrevocably destined
never to save a country from the horrors of an unjust war?
Whoever has pondered over the problems of the moral life
knows how easy it is for a dishonest conscience to elude the
most sacred truths and to render them powerless without
troubling to openly reject them. The application of moral
principles is often difficult and obscure. It requires a dis-
crimination which only an honest conscience can achieve.
A dishonest conscience is never embarrassed. Why bother,
for example, to attack the economic doctrine of the Church
on just price? Greedy merchants will always have plenty of
good reasons to prove that their profits conform perfectly
within the laws of just price. These arguments will be spe-
cious enough to convince many weak-willed people who pre-
fer not to examine the case too closely, lest they discover the
iniquity within their own consciences. Likewise, why bother
to openly declare that one rejects the teaching of the Church
on the conditions of a *just war*, and that makes a mockery of
justice with regard to it or anything else? It is much clev-
erer to profit by the obscurities which inevitably accompany
the application of a necessarily abstract doctrine. Using the
cover of darkness as a means of protection is a deceptive
method familiar to all marauders, pickpockets, and assassins.

In most cases the obscurity offers sufficient protection to the scoundrels. But there are typical cases where the application is comparatively clear; then the light of the doctrine itself becomes embarrassing and the only solution is to pass over the doctrine in silence. The encyclical *Divini Redemptoris* [On Atheistic Communism, 1937] notes that some employers objected to the encyclical *Quadragesimo Anno* [Forty Years After, 1931] being read publicly in their parishes. I was told that at the time of the Ethiopian war a theology professor in a Roman college felt very uneasy because his course included studying the theory of the just war. He consulted his religious superior who decided that current public opinion would not permit an academic treatment of so burning a political issue. All that can be said of such an omission is that it was incomparably less dishonest than the historical and doctrinal falsifications which had to be effected if the Fascist aggression was to be given the slightest appearance of justification.

The French had a very particular reason to oppose Fascist aggression in Ethiopia. It was clear that the success of this aggression would mean the complete collapse of the system of collective security with which France had great interest in strengthening. At the time the Italo-Ethiopian crisis began, the League of Nations had already experienced some resounding failures: the war in Manchuria (1932) and the withdrawal by Japan and Germany of their League of Nations memberships. Yet some recent events had given it a rather unexpected recovery of prestige: it had gained the adherence of Russia in 1934; it had successfully settled the quarrel between Hungary and Yugoslavia (1935) and it had maintained peace in the Saar district at the time of the plebiscite (January 1935). But above all, the League of Nations was supported at the time by extremely favorable public opinion in Great Britain. A political poll, the *Peace Ballot*, conducted by private organizations, showed that the great majority of British people had made up their minds in favor of a policy of complete fidelity to the Covenant, even going so far as to envisage the use of military sanctions. After a long and deplorable indecisive period, Great Britain showed herself determined to abandon her traditional policy of isolation and to fully commit herself to European and world affairs. She wanted however her commitments to have the recognized character of participation within a system of collective assistance.

In 1935 the League of Nations was strong enough to have stopped dead any intended Fascist aggression. On the other hand, it could not withstand another major failure. The Italo-Ethiopian conflict was to be the decisive test. The enemies of international law perfectly understood that.

In addition to the obligation of defending justice and of assuring the triumph of international order, France had another vital interest in maintaining their policy with Great Britain. England was her indispensable ally in a possible war with Nazi Germany, whose military power was augmenting daily. The era of the ill-fated policy of appeasement had not yet begun. British statesmen supported by an almost unanimous popular movement had understood the meaning of the aggression launched by Italy against people without defensive air power and artillery. They had understood that the establishment of a Fascist empire in East Africa would inevitably create a formidable and perhaps fatal threat to the route to the Indies and the British positions in the Eastern Mediterranean. As I write these lines, a hard battle is raging in Libya. What is happening today was foreseen as early as 1935. Those who are astonished that some Frenchmen are trying to drag France into the struggle against

Great Britain are ignorant of contemporary history. They know nothing of the decisive events which occurred in 1935 and 1936.

French foreign policy was controlled by Pierre Laval, whose true character has now been completely revealed by recent developments. To those people who considered only the official attitude of the French government, it might seem that its policy was wholly true to its commitments under the Covenant of the League of Nations. Before the beginning of hostilities, Laval joined his efforts to those of the British government in order to secure a peaceful settlement. Once the Italian aggression started, the Council of the League of Nations, in which France had a permanent seat, unanimously declared that Italy had resorted to war, contrary to her pledges. In the Assembly of the League, France joined in the unanimous vote in favor of the application of sanctions against Italy.

In fact, nobody ever believed in the integrity of this official policy. Laval was known to be a friend of Fascist Italy and his being in power seemed quite reassuring to those who had undertaken to sabotage international order. Friends and adversaries of Laval alike recognized that it was thanks to him that the League's sanctions had become a farce. These sanctions would have been effective in a long war, but the Fascists did not need a long war. Their aviators, with an extensive use of mustard gas, opened a road to Addis Ababa and then their columns marched on amidst the corpses. Mussolini appeared once again on the balcony of the Palazzo Venezia in Rome and declared that the war was over. The Ethiopian war was not over, but the first objective of the dictators was achieved. Europe was now disorganized, demoralized, and no longer had anything to fear from international collective security.

Laval is nothing more than a politician of the lowest order, a corporation lawyer, and a clever schemer who made a lot of money. The interesting thing to consider is the reaction of the French public to the challenge of the Ethiopian war to justice, international order, and the security of all nations. Few people then were so stupid as to fail to recognize the seriousness of the events. France split into supporters and adversaries of the League of Nations just as she had split, thirty-five years earlier, into supporters and adversaries of Captain Dreyfus. The adversaries of Mussolini were the men of the newly formed People's Front and a great number of Catholics. The Right, the conservatives and reactionaries, the nationalist party, whose members I have described as the *guardians of the city*, stood up almost unanimously against the League of Nations, international law, and the treaties signed by France. They supported the Italian aggression with feverish enthusiasm. Their excuse offered to patriots was that opposition to the ambitions of Fascist Italy would force her into an alliance with Germany. In fact, a resolute action against the Fascist aggression would have simply brought about the downfall of Mussolini's regime and the emergence of a republican Italy in which Nazi Germany could not have found an ally. This is precisely what they wanted to avoid at any price: the overthrow of this Fascist regime which they considered so much better than the French Republic—a regime which they had vainly tried to establish in France and which they would someday succeed in establishing through the defeat of the French armies. In any case the desire to maintain friendly relations with Italy could neither justify nor explain the enthusiasm with which this obviously unjust and cruel war was cheered on by Rightist parties and their sympathizers. Their zeal was above all a tribute to triumphant force, consistently accompanied by a diabolical irony in which were combined a contempt for the pledged word, a hatred of juridical forms, and an exaltation of violent passions at the expense of justice and mercy.

Patriotic considerations carried little weight amidst this explosion of wicked instincts. The few members of the Right who raised their voices in protest against the Italian aggression, either for moral reasons (François Mauriac) or for patriotic reasons (Pertinax [André Géraud] and Émile Buré) were soon disavowed by their parties, or left them in disgust. The Ethiopian war did more than anything else to convince many Catholics to break their traditional ties with the Right. These Catholics were to become the object of bitter resentment. A bishop told one of them a few years later: "They have not forgiven you your Christian attitude with regard to the Ethiopian war."

We then witnessed a strange orgy of vile passions. A large part of the French press was obviously bought out by the Italian government. To reinforce its propaganda, a group of well-known intellectuals, including a good number of French Academy stars, published a manifesto boldly entitled, *For the Defense of the West.*[2] As the title suggests, this manifesto contained nothing but lies and nonsense, but the celebrated authority of the signers could not fail to impress a great number of ill-informed and cowardly people. Those who were most willing to recall the German atrocities of 1914 had no objection to the extermination of the Ethiopian populace with mustard gas. The same groups who were quick to condemn the 1914 words of Chancellor Theobald von Bethmann-Hollweg, who called the treaty guaranteeing Belgian neutrality "a scrap of paper," now offered their sympathy to the Italian Fascist government tearing up scraps of paper in support of their so-called Ethiopian war of "civilization."[3]

I have tried to point out in the preceding pages three great reasons why the French should have unanimously opposed the Italo-Ethiopian War: justice, collective assistance, and Anglo-French cooperation were at stake. There were so many reasons why the French Right was to favor the Ethiopian war. Justice seemed to it an abstract and suspicious idea. It hated the League of Nations. It hated England. The great insulting campaign hurled against England by its newspapers was the logical complement to its campaign in favor of the Fascists. It was the time when the pamphleteer Henri Béraud published in *Gringoire* articles with such titles as "Why I Hate the English" and "Should England Be Reduced to Slavery?" Five years later, in his address announcing the Armistice, Marshal Pétain pointed out that France had not had enough allies.

Everyone recognized that this statement contained a bitter criticism of England. But the marshal could not afford to say that his most fervent supporters were among the men who, in regard to the question of war debts, plastered posters all over Paris demanding *"Not a cent for America,"* and who, in regard to the Ethiopian war, spoke of reducing England to slavery. This point must be made perfectly clear. The policy of stabbing England in the back, which is practiced today by Admiral François Darlan,[†] is only the fulfillment of a sort of oath taken in an atmosphere of hatred by the French Right in 1935.

The fate of Europe was really sealed during 1935 and 1936. Everything happened then as if the enemies of peace had accepted the fundamental assumption of the defenders of international institutions, namely, that international order could be guaranteed only by a system of collective assistance. Owing to the sabotage of the League of Nations, a new era was about to begin in which law would no longer be made by assemblies of jurists but by the force of arms as in the case of Ethiopia. Toward the end of 1935 the Parisian magazine *Le Document* published a special issue devoted to the pressing problem of rearmament. On the first page was an article accompanied by a picture of cloudy skies. The title was "We have lived for fifteen years in the clouds." For fifteen years Europe had been spared from exhausting herself with military expenditures. The article showed that this period had come to an end, and that in the new era which was beginning, *force* was to play a much greater role. The author frankly rejoiced over this change in international mores. We have lived in the clouds for fifteen years but now owing to universal rearmament life will begin in earnest again. The author of the article was General Maxime Weygand.[5]

What would happen if France were surpassed by rival nations in a world rearmament race? It could not be said that such a possibility was out of the question, but it was suggested that there could be no serious danger as long as the strong men in whom the nationalist party had placed its confidence remained in power. Who were these trusted men? Imagine for a moment the following parlor game in 1935 or 1936. A group of politically well-informed people amuse themselves by drawing up, on their own, a list of political men who have the confidence of "nationalist France." These lists would have varied considerably because the real answer was unclear. Yet one name at least would have appeared on all of them, that of Pierre Laval.

No doubt it was vaguely recognized that *in fact* the balance of military power had a great chance of being broken to the disadvantage of France. It was also known that *in fact* the "nationalist" party and Laval would not always remain in power. Thus, should a catastrophe occur, they would in any case have the consolation of saying that it was the fault of the Socialists, and that everything would have turned out differently if instead of trusting "this dirty Blum," France had kept on being guided by the wonderful Monsieur Laval. I know a few Frenchmen who relished this consolation after the defeat of France in June 1940.

APPENDIX 2

Manifestos and Documents

MANIFESTO OF FRENCH INTELLECTUALS
FOR THE DEFENSE OF THE WEST

(Manifeste des intellectuels français pour la défense
de l'Occident et la paix en Europe)

Le Temps (4 October 1935), Paris

Ed. note: The first wave of signers included some twelve members of the Académie française. The final list of over one thousand, according to Henri Massis, included nearly half the members of the Académie (see Jean-François Sirinelli, *Intellectuels et passions françaises: Manifestes et pétitions aux xxᵉ siècle* [Paris: Gallimard, 1990], 159 n. 1). A number of the signers were later elected to the Académie, including Charles Maurras (1938) as well as Massis himself (1960), although Maurras and others, such as Marshal Philippe

Pétain and Abel Bonnard, had their seats declared "vacated" at the liberation of France.

* * *

At a time when Italy is threatened with sanctions that may very well unleash a war without precedent, we, as French intellectuals, insist on declaring before the entire world that we wish to have nothing to do with these sanctions or this war.

This refusal is imposed on us not only by our gratitude toward a nation that has contributed to the defense of our invaded homeland: it is our very vocation that imposes it.

When the actions of men, who are responsible for the destiny of nations, risk putting the future of civilization in peril, those who have consecrated their labors to intellectual concerns owe it to themselves to make their voices heard in the defense of the human spirit.

There are those who strive to turn the people of Europe against Rome.

They do not hesitate to declare Italy guilty and, before all the world, to point to it as the common enemy—under the pretext of protecting in Africa the independence of an amalgam of uncivilized tribes, which in this way they would like to describe as great States gathered together in a fenced field.

By the offense of this monstrous coalition, the just interests of the Western community would be damaged, all civilization would be reduced to the position of the vanquished. Even to envision such a thing is already the sign of a mental illness, which betrays a veritable surrender of the civilizing spirit.

Intelligence itself—in those cases where it has not yet abdicated its authority—refuses all complicity in such a catastrophe. In addition, the undersigned consider themselves obliged to rise up against so many causes of death, which will wreck definitive ruin on the most precious part of our universe, and which will menace not only the lives, the material and spiritual goods of thousands of individuals, but even the very notion of *man*, the legitimacy of his possessions and his titles—all of which things the West until now has considered as superior and to which it owes its historic grandeur along with its creative virtues.

On this very notion, in which the West incarnates its ideals, its honors, its humanity, great peoples, like England, like France, have founded the most fruitful expressions of their vitality, as a justification of their work of colonization, which remains one of their most exalted. And would not these great powers be obliged immediately to abdicate their own colonial mission, if they wished, without deception, to forbid Rome from pursuing the same in those regions of Africa, in which it has a long time ago acquired incontestable rights, the accomplishment of the plans which it has honestly formulated and openly prepared?

In addition, is it possible without stupor to look upon a people, whose colonial empire covers one fifth of the globe, rise in opposition to the justifiable enterprises of a young Italy, and rashly adopt such a dangerous fiction as the absolute equality of all nations—something which, by the way, gains for them the support of all those revolutionary forces which lay claim to the same ideology to combat the internal regime of Italy and at the same time deliver Europe to the upheavals they seek.

It is to this disastrous alliance that Geneva offers its dangerous alibis for a false juridical universalism, which places on the same basis of equality the superior and the inferior, the civilized and the barbarian. Before our very eyes we have the results of this mania to equalize, which mixes everything together; because it is in its name that sanctions are formulated, sanctions which, in order to put obstacles in the way of a civilizing conquest of one of the most backward countries of the world (where Christianity itself has had no effect), would not hesitate to unleash a universal war, to form a coalition of all the anarchies, all forms of disorder, against a nation in which for fifteen years now some of the essential virtues of the highest forms of humanity have been affirmed, organized and fortified.

This fratricidal conflict would be not only a crime against peace, but also an unpardonable attack on the civilization of the West, that is to say, against the only valid future, which, today as in the past, lies open to the human race. As intellectuals, who have the obligation to protect culture with all the more vigilance since we profit more from its benefits, we cannot let civilization choose against itself. To prevent such a suicide, we appeal to all the forces of the human spirit.

—TRANS. BERNARD DOERING,
*Department of Romance Languages
and Literatures, University of Notre Dame*

This manifesto was initially signed by the following sixty-four prominent French right-wing intellectuals:

Maurice Donnay, Abel Hermant de Nolhac, Henry Bordeaux, Louis Madelin, Georges Lecomte, Édouard Estaunié, Louis Bertrand, André Chaumeix, Abel Bonnard, André Bellessort, Claude Farrère, (Académie française) Charles Benoist (l'Institut), Jacques Boulenger, Auguste Bailly, Gabriel Boissy, Maurice Bedel, Binet-Valmer, Louis

Brun, René Benjamin, René Bebaine, Robert Brasillach, Dr. Raymond Bernarp, H. Boegnar, Frances de Croisset, M. Constantine-Weyer, Paul Chack, Gaston Chérau, Lucien Copechot, Ch.-M. Chenu, Léon Daudet, Georges Deherme, Pierre Drieu de la Rochelle, Alfred Droin, Ch. Delvert, Prof. Louis Dunoyer, Bernard Fay (Collège de France), Albert Flament, Dr. Ch. Fiessinger, Jean Fayard, Jean Héritier, Robert Kemp, G. Le Cardonnel, Pierre Lafue, François Le Grix, Maurice Martin du Card, Gabriel Marcel, André Maurel, Camille Mauclair, Charles Maurras, Charles Méré, Henri Martineau, Henri Massis, Michel Missoffe, Claude Morgan, Léon Mirman, Jean-Pierre Maxence, Edmond Pilon, Prof. Charles Richet, André Rousseax, Édouard Schneider, Thierry Maulnier, Gonzague Truc, Pierre Valrillon, Robert Vallery Radot.

In the days following the original publication of the *Manifesto for the Defense of the West, Le Temps*, beginning on 5 October 1935, published new lists of additional signatories including:

Jean de Fabrègues, Cardinal Alfred Baudrillart [Académie française and recteur of l'Institut catholique de Paris], Henri Béraud, Alphonse de Châteaubriant, Pierre Mac-Orlan, Henri Ghéon, André Demaison, Pierre Mauriac, Pierre Gaxotte, Georges Grappe, Auguste Louis Barbillon (École de Beaux-arts), Marcel Aymé, Georges Blond, André Maurois, Maurice Denis . . . etc.

RESPONSE TO THE MANIFESTO [FOR THE DEFENSE
OF THE WEST] OF THE FASCIST INTELLECTUALS

(Réponse au manifeste des intellectuels fascistes)

Le Populaire (5 October 1935), *L'Œuvre* (5 October 1935),
La Croix (19 October 1935), Paris

Ed. note: Some scholars and translators have cited this material as *Manifeste pour le respect de la loi internationale* (*Manifesto for the Respect of International Law*).

* * *

On the very day of the bombardment of Adowa, on the day when the counting of the dead from the first battle began, several hundred people, including a certain number of intellectuals, who had gathered at the Maison de la Culture, were made aware of the manifesto entitled *For the Defense of the West*. It was published in the 4 October 1935 edition of *Le Temps*, with the signatures of sixty-four French intellectuals. Oddly this manifesto takes unfair advantage of the friendship of the French people for the Italian people, as well as of the "notion of the West" and the notion of "intelligence"; this is an attempt to misappropriate our nation's love for peace, in favor of a war under its most odious form, a war of aggression.

The undersigned have an altogether different conception of the real friendship that unites the people of France and Italy, and of the role that French intelligence must play in the present circumstances. They are astounded to find from

French pens the affirmation of the inequality of human races before the law, an idea so contrary to our tradition, and so insulting in itself to so many members of our community.

They find it deplorable that, at the very time when the League of Nations [S.D.N.] has justified its existence in the eyes of all men of good will, sixty-four intellectuals of our nation should launch against this Geneva institution an attack whose impertinence rivals its lack of substance. They are persuaded that these sixty-four intellectuals are far, far away from the real opinion and feeling of the masses of our people. Despite the action of a certain segment of the press whose motives appear far from being purely disinterested, the latter certainly know how to discern the true mission of the peoples of the West, and will refuse to misconstrue, as they are invited to do, the noble attitude of the English people and of their intellectuals. They consider it the duty of the French government to join in the efforts of all those governments who are struggling for peace and the [respect of international law].

They desire that the true representatives of French intelligence in the eyes of France and of the world here make their voices heard without delay.

—TRANS. BERNARD DOERING,
*Department of Romance Languages
and Literatures, University of Notre Dame*

The original signatories of the *l'Œuvre* publication of this anti-Fascist manifesto were:

Jules Romains, Luc Durtain, Adrienne Monnier, Louis Aragon, Léon Moussinac, Paul Poiret, Hussel (député de l'Israël), Frans Masereel, Paul Castiaux, Jean Effel, René Bloch, Georges Friedmann, Paul-Émile Bécat, Marcel Villard, Grandjean, Gérard Servèze, and 209 others.

They were joined later by the following writers, artists, and intellectuals:

André Gide, Romain Rolland, Jean Cassou, Claude Aveline, André Chamson, Amédée Ozenfant, Jean Guéhenno, André Ullmann, Jacques Kayser, Louis Martin-Chauffier, René Lalou, Pierre Gérôme, Alain, Perrin, Langevin, Paul Rivet, Fournier, Wurmser, Georges Boris, Robert Lange, Pierre de Lanux, Gabriel Delâtre, Charles Vildrac, Jean Prévost, Marcelle Auclair, Jean Carlu, André Malraux, Louis Guilloux, Paul Nizan, Pierre Unik, Paul Vaillant-Couturier, Emmanuel Bove, Emmanuel Mounier, Jacques Madaule, Marc Bernard, Roger Breuil, Denis de Rougemont, Robert Honnert, Jules Rivet, Léopold Chauveau, Jean Schlumberger, Louis Terrenoire, André Beucler, Louis Cheronnet, Georges Pillement, Benjamin Crémieux, André Cuisenier, Lévy-Bruhl, Hadamard, M. Alexandre, Jean-Richard Bloch, Pierre Brossolette, Madeleine Le Verrier, Elie Faure.

They were also joined by the 8,500 members of the Committee for the Vigilance of Anti-Fascist Intellectuals. See Jean-François Sirinelli, *Intellectuels et passions françaises: Manifestes et pétitions au xxᵉ siècle* (Paris: Gallimard, 1990), 156–57.

CONCERNING THE ITALO-ETHIOPIAN CONFLICT:
MANIFESTO FOR JUSTICE AND PEACE

(À propos du conflit italo-ethiopien: Manifeste pour
la justice et la paix)

Initially in *7 "Sept"—l'Hebdomadaire du Temps Présent* [Paris] 2ᵉ année,
no. 86 (18 October 1935): 5. Subsequently in the following
Parisian media: *L'Aube / Quotidien du Matin* 4ᵉ année, no. 1029
(18 October 1935): 1; *La Vie Catholique* 12ᵉ année, no. 517
(19 October 1935): 3; *La Croix* 56ᵉ année, no. 16157 (19 October 1935): 5;
Le Figaro 110ᵉ année, no. 293 (20 October 1935): 4; *Esprit* 4ᵉ année,
no. 38 (1 November 1935): 307–8

In the present confusion of minds, and in the face of the
serious situation created by the Italo-Ethiopian conflict, it
is impossible for those who refuse all at once to allow the
darkening of the principle of conscience and to admit the
hypothesis of a new European war, to remain silent.

The question in no way concerns the sympathies or an-
tipathies that one may have in regard to the internal regime
of Italy; it concerns justice and eternal values of which no
one can be uninterested.

No more is the question to know if the needs of a young
and active people for expansion have been sufficiently respected up to the present time. It is to know if these needs
justify the war. Neither the need to expand nor the task of
civilization it brings about has ever given one the right to
seize someone else's territories and bring death to them. It is
quite true that peoples who have arrived at a higher degree
of culture have a mission to help others, but it is a mockery

to call upon this mission of assistance in order to launch a war of conquest and prestige.

However, justice must be respected in all its demands. It is justice itself that requires that one be opposed to any extension of armed conflict.

A new European war would be an irreparable disaster. It is not because we refuse to give our approval to Mussolini that we are ready to accept such a misfortune. The generalization of the conflict would not only be a calamity for civilization and for the whole world. It would also be another iniquity this time in regard to the peoples who would find themselves implicated in this tragedy. It is a duty to come to the assistance of those who suffer injustice, but the strictest political morality never requires a people to resort for that reason to means that would entail its own loss or a universal disaster. It is to other means then that one must appeal. It should be recognized as a fact that the world is powerless to intervene by armed force in the Italo-Ethiopian conflict without rushing into even greater evils. It should never be forgotten either that it is a great injustice, even in the name of the law, to plunge a people into despair. But no force in the world can constrain the conscience for all that to find evil good, and good evil.

We do not deny the importance of the colonial task achieved by European states, and we know that it cannot be wiped out without a huge loss for humanity. But we also know that it has not been achieved without serious mistakes. And at the moment when Europe began to become better aware of its responsibilities toward people of color, and the conditions of justice and freedom toward which the system of colonization must evolve; we must consider as a moral disaster that "the benefits of Western colonialism" be shown to these people, with an unequalled outburst, by the superiority of its means of destruction placed at the service of violence, and with that one maintains that the violations of right of which such a war witnesses become venial under the pretext that it is a matter of a colonial enterprise. It is Western civilization itself that is threatened here, and the more we are attached to it, the more we feel bound to protest against the morals which make it abdicate its highest reason for being and which are fit to make it hateful worldwide.

It is also important to denounce the sophism of racial inequality. If one wants to say that certain races or certain nations are found in a less advanced cultural state than others, one simply observes an obvious fact. But one proceeds from there to the implicit assertion of an essential inequality which would delegate certain races or nations to be at the service of others, and which would change the laws of the just and the unjust in regard to them. That is pure paganism. Christianity makes us understand and realize this truth of the natural order that justice is owed to men without partiality, neither of race nor of nation, and that the soul and life of a black is as sacred as that of a white person. Already many men have found a cruel death in this war. Italian deaths and Abyssinian deaths, the Christian heart includes them all in fraternal compassion.

If the meaning of the just and the human is insufficient here to touch hearts at least the consideration of this West that one tries with such thoughtlessness to connect with a bad cause should induce every reflective mind to dread the use that other violent men can make of these very doctrines of the inequality of races, and of the meaninglessness of breaches of international commitments.

Current events show in a terribly clear way that the Geneva organization [the League of Nations] can be truly useful to world order only if peoples and governments sincerely want justice and peace. It is this will for justice and peace, taken together, that matters more than ever to assert today.

—TRANS. RALPH NELSON,
Department of Political Science,
University of Windsor, Canada

Signed by:

Joseph A. Georges, Chanoine Charles J. Alleaume, Fr. Bernard Allo, Jeanne Amcelet-Hustache, Paul Archambault, Fernand Aubrier, éditeur, Chanoine Gustave Bardy, Marie-Vincent Bernadot, O.P., Directeur de le *La Vie Intellectuelle* et de 7 *"Sept"* Georges Bertier, directeur de l'École des Roches, Georges Bidault, professeur agrégé de l'université, Étienne Borne, A. Boissard, Charles Du Bos, Maurice Brillant, Maurice Carite, Abbé Paul Catrice, Paul Cazin, Paul Chanson, Paul Claudel, Dr. Robert Cornilleau, Joseph Danel, E. Dermenghem, C. Devivaise, P. Dumaine, Maurice Eble, Joseph Folliet, Dr. de Fresquet, Stanislas Fumet, Maurice de Gandillac, Francisque Gay, André George, Marcel Griaule, Mgr. Gry, Georges Hoog, Pierre-Henri Simon, Georges Hourdin, Francis Jammes, Régis Jolivet, Louis Jouvet, Jean Lacroix. Maurice Lacroix, Céline Luotte, Jacques Madaule, Roland Manuel, Abbé Macquart, Jacques Maritain, L. Martin-Chauffier, François Mauriac, Edward Montier, Yves R. Simon, professeur à l'université catholique de Lille, Emmanuel Mounier, Ernest Pezet, Marc Sangnier, Gaston Tessier, André Therive, Abbé A. Vincent, J. Zamanski, Jacques Zeiller, L. Blanchaert, Jacques Copeau, A. Debray, Georges Desvallières, A-M. Goichon, J. Graff, Fr. Gratin, O.M.C.,

C. Grillet, Charles Grolleau, Henri Guillmin, François Henri, Joseph Hours, Pierre Humbert, A. Imbert, Abbé Daniel. Lallement, Mgr. Lavarenne, Chanoine Magnin, Yves Mainguy, Joseph Malegur, Chanoine Eugène Masure, Henri de Nolrac, Louis-Alfred Pages, Jean Peyraube, Chanoine L. Pirot, Marcel Poimboeuf, Mme. Tasset-Nissole, Abbé Thellier de Poncheville, Maurice Blondel, Marie Gasquet, Henriette Psichari.

An Open Letter Signed by a
Group of French Writers

(Une lettre d'un groupe [French] d'ecrivains pour la
justice et la paix des intellectuels et ecrivains catholiques)

————

L'Aube (23 October 1935), *Le Populaire* (23 October 1935),
7 "Sept" (25 October 1935), Paris

The undersigned writers, after having become aware of the
courageous manifesto *For Justice and Peace* that appeared in
different newspapers on October 18th consider that it is timely
to ask you to join their signatures to those of your friends.
They see the assertion of principles which should serve as a
basis for an examination of the problem that present events
impose on our conscience nobly expressed in your manifesto.
We are bound to emphasize with you the necessity, above all,
of upholding the idea and the will of justice, and we completely
give our approval to your declarations in this regard. This assertion of the will to justice seems to us of the highest importance and to our view overrides any other consideration.

—TRANS. RALPH NELSON,
Department of Political Science,
University of Windsor, Canada

Among the signatories:

André Gide, Julien Benda, André Chamson, Jean Chamson, Jean Cassou, Léopold Chauveau, André Viollis, Jacques Chabannes, Jean Schulmberger, Claude Aveline, Roger Martin du Gard, Jean Guéhenno, Henry de Montherlant.

An Open Letter from Gabriel Marcel

(Une Lettre de M. Gabriel Marcel)

7 *"Sept"* (25 October 1935), Paris

Ed. note: Although Gabriel Marcel was no Fascist, nonetheless he signed the *Manifesto for the Defense of the West*. Three weeks later he published the following "open letter" in explanation of why he had signed. His letter is of value for an understanding of the complexities of the developing crisis and the battle of the manifestos in France during the 1930s. It should be noted that Marcel supported the efforts of more liberal intellectuals and their subsequent manifestos regarding the Spanish Civil War (see chap. 10 n. 2). The following is the English version of his letter.

*   *   *

I find myself—undoubtedly through my own fault—in the rather painful paradoxical situation of being unable to add my signature to a manifesto which appeared in this very same newspaper last week and whose spirit and tenor I support—because I signed another text to which I gave no more than a pragmatic adherence. It goes without saying that the nationalist, Occidentalist and colonialist ideology which permeates the "Manifesto of the Sixty-four" [*Manifesto for the Defense of the West*] in no way corresponds to my own way of thinking. But I thought, at the precise moment when this text was sent to me, that I did not have to take account of these differences, however serious they might have been, and that the only important thing was to join with those who refused categorically to admit that France could let itself be dragged into an armed conflict along with Italy at the time of its Ethiopian expedition. As far as I am concerned, I support this refusal without hesitation. But I deplore the fact that this has been interpreted as a kind of absolution for an act of aggression that legitimate Italian aspirations certainly in no way justify. I have been profoundly saddened to learn that my signature had surprised many of my friends and had given them the impression that I am today a convert to theses that I formally repudiate. The conclusion I draw from this episode is that one does not have the right to sign a text for purely pragmatic reasons; that is to say, if one cannot subscribe in detail to each of the assertions it includes. I thought that there was in it a vital interest that took precedence over any intellectual consideration—and today I believe that this was in fact an illicit distinction. This is the kind of *mea culpa* that I feel obliged in all simplicity to make public here.

The time is ripe, alas! for an examination of conscience. It seems evident to me that hypocrisies—all hypocrisies—are subjected today to the chastisement they deserve. Would it not be honest to recognize that all too often some mental reservation accompanied the adherence that many of us have given to the principles of the League of Nations, or that we, the French in particular, have seen it indeed, not as an end in itself, but rather as a precious instrument to be maintained, to be kept in top condition in the face of an aggression of which we ourselves might be the object? Today when we are not directly threatened, we tend to disown these principles because the adherence we gave them was formal, and in reality conditional. Remarks of the same kind would certainly have to be made with regard to England.

And we would have to go much further and ask ourselves if there wasn't a universal act of hypocrisy in the pretense of establishing a League of Nations at a time when the moral conscience of those nations was still at a rudimentary stage, something that contemporary events oblige us to recognize. Perhaps we believed that the League of Nations would develop this moral conscience: I am not sure that history, up till the present, may not have cruelly given the lie to this hope. May this present crisis, if by chance a catastrophe can be avoided, oblige us all finally to face up to certain embarrassing truths . . . It is only on this pre-requisite condition that we can hope, according to the wishes of all men of good will, to bring to effective realization what, in many regards, is still nothing more, alas! than a sham.

Gabriel Marcel

—TRANS. BERNARD DOERING,
*Department of Modern Languages
and Literatures, University of Notre Dame*

NOTES

1. In 1894 Alfred Dreyfus, a French Army captain who also happened to be Jewish, was convicted of spying for Germany, for treason, and sentenced to Devil's Island prison. When Émile Zola espoused the cause of Dreyfus in his famous open letter "J'accuse" published in Clemenceau's newspaper *l'Aurore* (13 January 1898), evidence then came to light that he was innocent. The true traitor was a certain Major Charles Ferdinand Walsin-Esterhazy. France split into two passionate factions for and against Dreyfus. The affair also profoundly reflected anti-Semitic and pro-Jewish elements in French society. For a brilliant treatment of this French crisis see Hannah Arendt, *The Origins of Totalitarianism* (New York: Harcourt Brace & Co., 1951), chap. 4 "The Dreyfus Affair," 89–120. [Rev. note]

2. Yves R. Simon, *Introduction à l'ontologie du connaître* (Paris: Desclée de Brouwer, 1934; reprint, Dubuque, IA: Wm. C. Brown, 1965), English trans., *An Introduction to Metaphysics of Knowledge*

(New York: Fordham University Press, 1990); *Critique de la connaissance morale* (Paris: Desclée de Brouwer, 1934), English trans.,
A Critique of Moral Knowledge (New York: Fordham University
Press, 2002); *Trois leçons sur la travail* (Paris: Pierre Téqui, 1938);
and scores of articles. [Ed. note]

CHAPTER ONE
FROM BEFORE THE WAR TO THE STRESA CONFERENCE

1. Italy, Germany, and Austria-Hungary formed the Triple Alliance in 1882. The Italians signed the treaty with the other two
nations in part because it was displeased by French opposition to
Italian efforts at colonization. [Ed. note]

2. Alsace-Lorraine, a traditional French territory situated on
the Eastern border with Germany, was often a pawn in struggles
between the two nations. In 1871 a newly united Germany defeated
France in the Franco-Prussian War and annexed the territory;
some French sympathized with Italy because they saw parallels
in its own territorial claims. In 1919 the territory reverted back to
France. [Ed. note]

3. Caporetto is a stretch of land on Italy's borders. Austrian and
German forces took its weak defense forces by surprise, forced a
retreat, and captured the region on the date indicated. [Ed. note]

4. The Treaty of London was secretly signed on 26 April 1915
by France, Russia, Great Britain, and Italy. It determined wartime
activity support between the Allies, and the allocation of disputed
lands. [Ed. note]

5. Ernest Lémonon, *La Politique coloniale de l'Italie* (Paris: Felix
Alcan, 1919), 74.

6. Ernest Lémonon, *L'Italie d'apres-guerre* (Paris: Felix Alcan,
1922), 91.

7. In Stresa, Italy, Great Britain, France, and Italy pledge to
sustain a united front against German rearmament, which would
violate the Treaty of Versailles. [Ed. note]

CHAPTER TWO
WHAT DO WE CARE ABOUT ETHIOPIA?

1. *Manifesto of French Intellectuals for the Defense of the West* (*Manifeste des intellectuels français pour la défense de l'Occident et la paix en Europe*). See appendix 2. [Ed. note]

2. It is clear that the patriotism of covetousness is often legitimate. What I want to observe here is that it represents an inferior kind of patriotism, one that threatens international order once it becomes preponderant.

CHAPTER FOUR
BUT IS THIS WAR JUST?

1. We emphasize the exceptional nature of such limited situations, which ought in addition to be verified by some authority or a judge.

2. *Manifesto of French Intellectuals for the Defense of the West.* See appendix 2. [Ed. note]

CHAPTER FIVE
ETHIOPIA'S FOREIGN RELATIONS

1. Note here that our perspective is not that of a historian. We want to examine some judgments, not to tell a story; but we cannot abstract from the history that constitutes the subject, or the occasion, for these judgments. In the historical configurations that we must examine, we will consider primarily or exclusively the formal aspects under which events present themselves directly to the judgment of political philosophy.

2. Negus is the Amharic word for king or ruler. Johannes IV was emperor of Ethiopia from 1872 until his death in 1889. [Ed. note]

3. Italo-Ethiopian Treaty of 1928, also known as the Italo-Ethiopian Treaty of Friendship. [Ed. note]

CHAPTER SIX
THE MAD DOG

1. Italo-Ethiopian Treaty of 1928. [Ed. note]

CHAPTER SEVEN
ETHIOPIA'S INTERNAL SITUATION

1. French General Pierre Étienne Cambronne commanded the Imperial Guard at Waterloo and was rumored to have said bravely, when asked to surrender, "The Guard dies, but it does not surrender." In another version he answered with a simple word of five letters [*merde*], called since then "Cambronne's word." The General, however, denied that.

CHAPTER EIGHT
THE COVENANT OF THE LEAGUE OF NATIONS

1. Indeed, the Italian plenipotentiaries had, on 20 May 1919, asked for the concession of Djibouti and of the Addis Ababa Railroad, in fulfillment of the London Accords.
2. Except for the embargo on provision of arms, a harmless measure for Italy, but a formidable one for Ethiopia.

CHAPTER NINE
BRITISH POLICY

1. In 1934 the British voted for "peace" in an informal poll and resolved not to resort to war to solve international problems.

CHAPTER TEN

THE INTERVENTION OF THE INTELLECTUALS

1. See the articles of Jean-Richard Bloch, "Pas un coup de canon," *L'Œuvre* (21 September 1935) and "La Gloire déshonoré," *L'Œuvre* (11 December 1935).

2. See in particular the explanations presented with a pleasant frankness by Gabriel Marcel in 7 *"Sept"* [Paris] (25 October 1935). [See appendix 2.]

3. Just after the publication of the *Manifesto for the Defense of the West*, a group of leftist writers published, in protest, a *Manifesto for Respect of International Law* [or, *Response to the Manifesto of the Fascist Intellectuals*] (5 October 1935); though this document did not find unanimous support among the opponents of the *Manifesto for the Defense of the West*. That was because it failed to express the need to avoid sanctions that would cause a further extension of the conflict, to safeguard in tandem both justice and peace. The omission was remedied in *Concerning the Italo-Ethiopian Conflict: Manifesto for Justice and Peace* (19 October 1935), which gained the support of numerous signers of the *Manifesto for Respect of International Law*. For the three manifestos see appendix 2. [Rev. note]

CHAPTER ELEVEN

REFLECTIONS ON CERTAIN RESISTANCES TO THE PROGRESS OF INTERNATIONAL LAW

1. The French government's notorious *Notebook B* was a black-list of potential national enemies and spies who were to be immediately arrested in the event of war. It was first created in 1886 and continuously updated thereafter.

2. Erich Marie Remarque, *All Quiet on the Western Front* (Boston: Little, Brown & Co. 1929); orig. pub. *Im Westen Nichts* (Berlin: Propyläen-verlag, 1929); French trans., *À l'ouest, rien de nouveau* (Paris: Stock, 1929). [Rev. note]

APPENDIX 1

ETHIOPIA REVISITED: *THE ROAD TO VICHY*

1. Let us recall here the strong statement of Pope Pius XI delivered at Castle Gandolfo in September 1935.

2. The full title was *Manifesto of French Intellectuals for the Defense of the West and Peace in Europe* (*Manifeste des intellectuels français pour la défense de l'Occident et la piax en Europe*). It was first published on 4 October 1935 in *Le Temps* (Paris). Henri Massis was one of its chief architects. See appendix 2. [Ed. note]

3. It is interesting to reread the speech in which Theobald von Bethmann-Hollweg announced to the Reichstag the invasion of Belgium at the onset of the Great War and to compare it with the manifesto *For the Defense of the West*. Compared with the average member of the French Academy, Bethmann-Hollweg appears as a man of scrupulous conscience. He took the trouble to recognize that the violation of Belgian neutrality was contrary to law. He took the time to express the intention of repairing the injustice which necessity, as he called it, compelled him to commit. The "defenders of the West" did not bother about such scruples. They were already ripe in 1935 for the policy of "collaboration" with the Nazis. [Rev. note]

4. François Darlan was Vichy's Admiral of the French fleet, vice-premier, and foreign minister. He was subsequently assassinated in Algeria in 1942 shortly after finally concluding an armistice with the Allies. [Ed. note]

5. General Maxime Weygand, French Army Chief of Staff. In 1940 his inexperience as a field commander led in part to the disastrous defense and route of the French army. [Ed. note]

BIBLIOGRAPHY

Arendt, Hannah. *The Origins of Totalitarianism.* New York: Harcourt, Brace & Co., 1951.

Berth, Édouard. *Guerre des États ou Guerre des classes.* Paris: Marcel Rivière, 1924.

Bloch, Jean-Richard. "Pas un coup de canon." *L'Œuvre* [Paris] (21 September 1935).

————. "La Gloire déshonoré." *L'Œuvre* [Paris] (11 December 1935).

Lémonon, Ernest. *La Politique coloniale de l'Italie.* Paris: Felix Alcan, 1919.

————. *Italie d'après-guerre.* Paris: Felix Alcan, 1922.

Proudhon, Pierre-Joseph. *La Guerre et la paix: Rescherches sur le principe et la constitution du droit des gens.* 2 vols. Paris: Michel-Lévy Frères, 1861.

Remarque, Erich Maria. *All Quiet on the Western Front.* Boston: Little, Brown & Co., 1929. Originally published as *Im Westen Nichts.* Berlin: Propyläen-verlag, 1929; French trans., *À L'ouest, rien de nouveau.* Paris: Stock, 1929.

Simon, Yves R. *Critique de la connaissance morale.* Paris: Desclée de Brouwer, 1934. English trans., *A Critique of Moral Knowledge.* New York: Fordham University Press, 2002.

———. *Introduction à l'ontologie du connaître.* Paris: Desclée de Brouwer, 1934. Reprint, Dubuque, IA: William C. Brown, 1965. English trans., *An Introduction to Metaphysics of Knowledge.* New York: Fordham University Press, 1990.

———. *La Campagne d'Éthiopie et la pensée politique française.* Lille: Société d'Impressions Littéraires, Industrielles et Commerciales, 1936. Second edition, Paris: Desclée de Brouwer, 1937.

———. *Trois leçons sur la travail.* Paris: Pierre Téqui, 1938.

———. *The Road to Vichy, 1918–1938.* Translated by James A. Corbett and George J. McMorrow. New York: Sheed & Ward, 1942. Revised with an introduction by John Hellman, Lanham, MD: University Press of America, 1988; reprint 1989. Originally published as *La Grande crise de la République française: Observations sur la vie politique des français de 1918 à 1938.* Problèmes Actuels. Montréal: Éditions de l'Arbre, 1941. [Appendix 1]

Sorel, Georges. *Reflections on Violence.* New York: Cambridge University Press, 1999. Originally published as *Réflexions sur la violence.* Paris: Marcel Rivière et cie., 1908.

Manifestos and Documents [Appendix 2]

Concerning the Italo-Ethiopian Conflict: Manifesto for Justice and Peace [À propos du conflict italo-ethiopien: Manifeste pour la justice et la paix]. La Croix [Paris] 56, no. 16157 (19 October 1935). Subsequently published in *L'Aube / Quotidien du Matin* [Paris] 4e année, no. 1029 (18 October 1935): 1; *La Vie Catholique* [Paris] 12ᵉ année, no. 517 (19 October 1935): 3; *La Croix* [Paris] 56ᵉ année, no. 16157 (19 October 1935): 5; *Le Figaro* [Paris] 110ᵉ année, no. 293 (20 October 1935): 4; *Esprit* [Paris] 4ᵉ année, no. 38 (1 November 1935): 307–8.

Manifesto of French Intellectuals for the Defense of the West [Manifeste des intellectuels français pour la défense de l'Occident et la paix en

Europe]. *Le Temps* [Paris] (4 October 1935). Signed by sixty-four prominent French intellectuals.

Marcel, Gabriel. *An Open Letter from Gabriel Marcel* [*Une lettre de M. Gabriel Marcel*]. *7 "Sept"—l'Hebdomadaire du Temps Présent* [Paris] 2ᵉ année (25 October 1935).

An Open Letter Signed by a Group of French Writers [*Une Lettre d'Un Groupe d'ecrivains pour la justice et la paix des intellectuels et ecrivains catholiques*]. *L'Aube* [Paris] (23 October 1935); *Le Populaire* [Paris] (23 October 1935); *7 "Sept"* [Paris] (25 October 1935).

Response to the Manifesto of French Intellectuals [*Réponse au manifeste des intellectuels fascistes*]. *Le Populaire* [Paris] (5 October 1935). Also cited as *Manifesto for the Respect of International Law* [*Manifeste pour le respect de la loi international*].

RELATED WORKS BY YVES R. SIMON

Jacques Maritain, Yves Simon: Correspondance. Vol. 1, *Les années françaises (1927–1940)*. Edited by Florian Michel in collaboration with Anthony O. Simon and René Mougel. Tours, France: Editions CLD (Cahiers, Livres, Disques), 2008. Pp. 460.

"À Propos de la guerre de Chine." *Univers—Bulletin Catholique International* [Lille / Paris] 4ᵉ année, no. 31 (March / April 1938): 24–26.

"Patriotisme." *Temps Présent* [Paris] 2ᵉ année, no. 23 (8 April 1938): 1.

"Faire de la politique." *Temps Présent* [Paris] 2ᵉ année, no. 34 (24 June 1938): 3.

"Crimes salutaires." *Temps Présent* [Paris] 2ᵉ année (22 July 1938): 1.

"Raison politique." *Temps Présent* [Paris] 2ᵉ année (29 July 1938): 1.

"L'Opinion américaine et la guerre d' Espagne." *L'Aube* [Paris] 8ᵉ année, no. 1965 (13 January 1939): 1.

"Liberty and Authority." In *Proceedings of the American Catholic Philosophical Association*. Vol. 16, *The Problem of Liberty*, 86–114. Washington, D.C.: American Catholic Philosophical Association, 1940.

"The European Crisis and the Downfall of the French Republic."
The Review of Politics [Notre Dame, IN] 3, no. 1 (January 1941):
32–64.

"Résolution" [To take a stand]. *France Forever* [New York] 1, no. 3
(January / February 1941): 3.

"France Under the Swastika." *The Commonweal* [New York] 33,
no. 24 (April 4, 1941): 590–92.

La Marche à la délivrance. Collection Civilisation. New York: Éditions de la Maison Française, 1942. English trans., *The March to
Liberation.* Milwaukee, WI: Tower Press, 1942.

"Chronique des événements internationaux: Saint Pierre et Mique-
lon." *La Nouvelle Relève* [Montréal] 1, no. 5 (February 1942):
303–6.

"La Guerre longue et la guerre dure." *La Nouvelle Relève* [Mon-
tréal] 1, no. 6 (March 1942): 354–59.

"Les Événements internationaux: L'offense du printemps." *La Nouvelle Relève* [Montréal] 1, no. 7 (April 1942): 428–35.

"La Paix de compromis: Les événements internationaux." *La Nouvelle Relève* [Montréal] 2, no. 1 (October 1942): 41–47.

"Una Guerra civil internacional." *Argentina Libre* [Buenos Aires]
(24 December 1942).

"France and the United Nations." *The Review of Politics* [Notre
Dame, IN] 5, no. 1 (January 1943): 26–37.

"Internal Policy of Liberated France: A World Problem." *France /
Canada* [Ottawa] (English edition) 2, no. 5 (May 1944): 6–7.

"La Politique intérieure de la France libérée: Problème mondial."
France / Canada [Ottawa] (French edition) 2, no. 5 (May 1944):
6–7.

"La Démocratie et le purisme démocratique." *La République Française* [New York] 1, no. 7 (August 1944): 6–9.

"La Démocratie et le purisme démocratique." *Supplément des Nou-
velles Catholiques* [Ottawa] no. 39 (1 October 1944): 1–3.

"Democracy and the Purists." *The Commonweal* [New York] 41,
no. 2 (October 27, 1944): 32–36.

"La Democracia y los puristas." *Orden Cristiano* [Buenos Aires]
año 4, no. 79 (15 December 1944): 709–12.

"Economic Organization in a Democracy." *Proceedings of the American Catholic Philosophical Association*. Vol. 20, *The Philosophy of Democracy*, 83–108. Washington, D.C.: American Catholic Philosophical Association, 1945.

Par delà l'expérience du désespoir. Montréal: Lucien Parizeau, 1945. Translated by Willard R. Trask as *Community of the Free*. New York: Henry Holt & Co.: 1947. Revised edition, Lanham, MD: University Press of America, 1984.

"Secret Sources of the Success of the Racist Ideology." *The Review of Politics* [Notre Dame, IN] 7, no. 1 (January 1945): 74–105.

"La Democracia y los puristas." *Politica y Espiritu* [Santiago de Chile] año 1, no. 1 (July 1945): 7–11.

Philosophy of Democratic Government. The Charles R. Walgreen Foundation Lectures. Chicago: University of Chicago Press, 1951. Revised edition, Notre Dame, IN: University of Notre Dame Press, 1993, reprint, 2007.

Practical Knowledge. Edited by Robert J. Mulvaney. New York: Fordham University Press, 1991.

EDITOR'S REFERENCE BIBLIOGRAPHY

Bars, Henry. "Gabriel Marcel et Jacques Maritain." In *Jacques Maritain et ses contemporains*, edited by Bernard Hubert and Yves Floucat, 231–54. Paris: Desclée, 1991.

Berman, Nathaniel A. "Beyond Colonialism and Nationalism? Ethiopia, Czechoslovakia, and Peaceful Change." *Nordic Journal of International Law* 65 (1996): 421–79.

Chenaux, Philippe. *Entre Maritain et Maurras: Une génération intellectuelle catholique (1920–1930)*. Paris: Les Éditions du Cerf, 1999.

Christophe, Paul. *1939–1940, les catholiques devant la guerre*. Paris: Les Éditions Ouvrières, 1989.

Coutrot, Aline. *Un Courant de la pensée catholique: L'Hebdomadaire "Sept" (Mars 1934–Août 1937)*. Preface by René Rémond. Paris: Les Éditions du Cerf, 1961. Revised edition published as *"Sept," Un Journal, un Combat: Mars 1934–Août 1937*. Paris: Éditions Cana, 1982.

Doering, Bernard. *Jacques Maritain and the French Catholic Intellectuals.* Notre Dame, IN: University of Notre Dame Press, 1983. See esp. chap. 3, "The Decade of Manifestos."

Fumet, Stanislas. *Histoire de Dieu dans ma vie: Souvenirs choisis.* Paris: Éditions Fayard / Mame, 1978.

Hellman, John. "The Anti-Democratic impulse in Catholicism: Jacques Maritain, Yves R. Simon and Charles de Gaulle during World War II." *Journal of Church and State* 33, no. 3 (Summer 1991): 453–71.

————. *Emmanuel Mounier and the New Catholic Left 1930–1950.* Toronto: University of Toronto Press, 1981.

Kuic, Vukan. *Yves R. Simon: Real Democracy.* Lanham, MD: Rowman & Littlefield, 1999.

L'Affaire Dreyfus: 1894–1908: A Chronology. A highly useful detailed weekly chronology of the events of the Dreyfus Affair. A thirteen-page text is available at www.19e.org/chronologie/affairedreyfus.htm.

Maritain, Jacques. *Jacques et Raïssa Maritain: Œuvres Complètes.* Vol. 6, 1935–1938. Paris: Éditions Saint-Paul, 1984.

Michelet, Edmond. *Rue de la liberté: Dachau 1943–1945.* Paris: Éditions du Seuil, 1955.

Prévotat, Jacques. *Les Catholiques et l'Action française: Histoire d'une condamnation 1899–1939.* Paris: Librairie Arthème Fayard, 2001.

Rauch, R. William, Jr. *Politics and Belief in Contemporary France: Emmanuel Mounier and Christian Democracy, 1932–1950.* The Hague: Martinus Nijhoff, 1972.

Rémond, René. *Les Crises du catholicisme en France dans les années trente.* Paris: Éditions Cana, 1996.

Simon, Anthony O., ed. *Acquaintance with the Absolute: The Philosophy of Yves R. Simon: Essays and Bibliography.* New York: Fordham University Press, 1998. The volume contains "Yves R. Simon: A Definitive Bibliography, 1923–1996," 185–305, compiled and annotated by Anthony O. Simon with a bibliographic index.

Sirinelli, Jean-François. *Intellectuels et passions françaises: Manifestes et pétitions au xxᵉ siècle.* Paris: Gallimard, 1990.

Thieulloy, Guilliame de. *Le Chevalier de l'absolu: Jacques Maritain entre mystique et politique.* Paris: Éditions Gallimard, 2005.

Weber, Engen. *Action Française: Royalism and Reaction in Twentieth-Century France.* Stanford, CA: Stanford University Press, 1962.

———. *The Hollow Years: France in the 1930s.* New York: W. W. Norton, 1994.

———. *L'Action française.* Paris: Librairie Arthème Fayard, 1985.

Winock, Michel. *Le Siècle des intellectuels.* Paris: Éditions du Seuil, 1999.

Yves R. Simon 1903–1961. Special Issue. *Cahiers Jacques Maritain* [Kolbsheim, France] 47 (December 2003). Pp. 128.

INDEX

Bebaine, René, 97
Bécat, Paul-Émile, 100
Bedel, Maurice, 96
Bellessort, André, 96
Benda, Julien, 24, 107
Beneš, Edvard, 61
Benjamin, René, 97
Benoist, Charles, 96
Béraud, Henri, 90
Bernadot, Marie-Vincent, O.P., 104
Bernard, Marc, 100
Bernarp, Raymond, 97
Berth, Édouard, 78
Bertier, Georges, 104
Bertrand, Louis, 96
Bethmann-Hollweg, Theobald von, 89, 116n3
Beucler, André, 100
Bidault, Georges, 104
Binet-Valmer, Jean, 96
Bismarck, Otto Eduard von, 39
Black Shirts, 33
Blanchaert, Léon, 104
Bloch, Jean-Richard, 100, 115n1 (chap. 10)
Bloch, René, 100
Blond, Georges, 97
Blondel, Maurice, 105
Blum, Léon, 92
Boegnar, Henri, 97
Boissard, André, 104
Boissy, Gabriel, 96
Bolshevism, 20
Bonnard, Abel, 94
Bordeaux, Henry, 96

Boris, Georges, 100
Borne, Étienne, 104
Boulenger, Jacques, 96
Bove, Emmanuel, 100
Brasillach, Robert, 97
Breuil, Roger, 100
Brillant, Maurice, 104
Brossolette, Pierre, 100
Brun, Louis, 97
Buré, Émile, 89

Cambronne, Pierre Étienne, 47, 114n1 (chap. 7)
Caporetto, battle of, 6–7, 112n3
Carite, Maurice, 104
Carlu, Jean, 100
Cassou, Jean, 100
Castiaux, Paul, 100
Catholic Church, 73, 84
Catrice, Abbé Paul, 104
Cazin, Paul, 104
Chabannes, Jacques, 107
Chack, Paul, 97
Chamson, André, 107
Chamson, Jean, 107
Chanson, Paul, 104
Châteaubriant, Alphonse de, 97
Chaumeix, André, 96
Chauveau, Léopold, 100, 107
Chenu, Ch.-M., 97
Chérau, Gaston, 97
Cheronnet, Louis, 100
Christian Democrats, 9
Claudel, Paul, 104
Clemenceau, Georges, 111n1
Conference of Stresa, 10, 49

YVES R. SIMON

(1903–1961)

was the author of twenty books

and professor of philosophy at

the University of Notre Dame

and the University of Chicago.

ANTHONY O. SIMON

is the director of

the Yves. R. Simon Institute.